XO

Praise for *Becoming Super Woman*

"*Becoming Super Woman* shows you taking care of yourself is not just OK but the only way to succeed."

—BOBBI BROWN, founder of Bobbi Brown Cosmetics

"Want it all? Who doesn't?! Nicole provides the secret sauce in *Becoming Super Woman*. It is a must-read for women looking to thrive in the workforce."

—BARBARA CORCORAN, founder of The Corcoran Group and investor on *Shark Tank*

"Nicole is the real deal. Her influence on women to get their finances and career in order is unparalleled. Now, she is helping a generation of women whose working-like-crazy is driving them crazy."

—REBECCA MINKOFF, founder of Rebecca Minkoff

"Like a confidence-boosting best friend, Nicole Lapin guides you through her own mental health journey while showing you how to channel your inner badass and still save time for yourself. *Becoming Super Woman* reminds us a hero lives inside all of us—even if we don't know it yet."

—PAIGE ADAMS-GELLER, founder of PAIGE

"Burnout is real. Nicole Lapin understands this firsthand, and the steps she lays out will help you become your most balanced, successful self."

—JULIA HARTZ, cofounder and CEO of Eventbrite

"To become super, we must first take care of ourselves, and we must set our own goals while setting aside unhelpful doubts. *Becoming Super Woman* reminds us that we can only define success from within."

—PAYAL KADAKIA, founder and CEO of ClassPass

"The professional women I know are all highly intelligent, ambitious, and career-driven. But we're not made of steel! Read this book to help master the degree of life and achieve more success than you ever thought possible."

—ROSIE O'NEILL, cofounder and co-CEO of Sugarfina

"Too many women are on the verge of burnout and breakdown. *Becoming Super Woman* is the only actionable guide to teach women how to thrive in a world that expects them to be Superwoman!"

—MINDY GROSSMAN, CEO of WW International

"*Becoming Super Woman* is a timely reminder that we can't afford to set our own well-being on the backburner. Nicole will help you build the confidence to follow your own gut and create a strong powerful masterpiece that is your life. Every one of us needs a copy."

—**JULIE SMOLYANSKY, CEO of Lifeway Foods**

"*Becoming Super Woman* reminds us that if we try to be all things to all people, we are nothing to no one. The only way to be of value to anyone else is to be of value to yourself first. Nicole's simple 12 steps get you back on track."

—**JODI GUBER BRUFSKY, founder and Chief Creative Officer of Beyond Yoga**

"There comes a time in everyone's life when we need a hero, and Nicole reminds us that the hero we seek has been inside of us all along. *Becoming Super Woman* enlightens and empowers in the smart signature voice of a truly super woman."

—**LIZ DEE, co-president of Smarties Candy Company**

"*Becoming Super Woman* should be mandatory reading for all women looking to succeed in their careers."

—**TRACY DINUNZIO, founder and CEO of Tradesy**

"*Becoming Super Woman* is truly eye-opening and inspiring! Nicole is a wonderful role model for women today, for opening up about such a personal struggle—one that so many of us can relate to. Take her guidance to heart, and it will change your life."

—**MARIAM NAFICY, founder and CEO of Minted**

"Nicole has done it again! Equal parts vulnerable and smartass Boss Bitch—just our cup of (organic) tea. These are valuable lessons about the importance of self-care, not just for personal wellness but for career success. Now, stop browsing the damn accolades and read the book!"

—**ZOË SAKOUTIS AND ERICA HUSS, founders of BluePrint**

"Nicole has done it again! Her honesty and realness will make you laugh and learn like you're hearing from your smart-ass best friend."

—**JASON FEIFER, editor in chief of *Entrepreneur Magazine***

Praise for Nicole Lapin and previous titles

"Trust her: She's been there."

—*GLAMOUR*

"Nicole Lapin is singularly qualified to demystify money for the millennial set . . . with a no nonsense chic style."

—*ELLE MAGAZINE*

"One of today's brightest young stars in media and a serial entrepreneur."

—*FETE LIFESTYLE MAGAZINE*

"Stressing over money and career can harm your overall health. Let Nicole be the doctor for your financial and business health, and you will feel better in more ways than you'd think."

—*DR. OZ*

"Nicole's advice is a swift kick in the pants to the young, ambitious, upstart women out there who want control over their lives, debts, and careers."

—*WENDY WILLIAMS*

"The role of women in the workforce is changing, and today women are disrupting the workplace - for the better. Ladies, it's time to disrupt your own industry. Nicole will show you how."

—*SARA BLAKELY, founder of Spanx*

"Nicole's advice is ON POINT! Here material and delivery is current, real, and entertaining."

—*LAVINIA ERRICO, founder of Equinox*

"Whether you want to branch out with your own startup or get ahead in your current job, Nicole knows just how to develop those skills to get you where you want to be. She's a perfect role model for young women."

—*BRIT MORIN, founder of Brit + Co.*

"If you're a woman and you like money, you need to read this book. Immediately. You can't afford to miss this one, ladies."

—*ALLI WEBB, founder of Drybar*

"Nicole does a fabulous job educating people about money while always keeping it fun and entertaining."

—ALEXIS MAYBANK, founder of Gilt Groupe

"At last! A book that's cool enough for my kick-ass teenage daughters, and smart enough for my CEO self!"

—JULIE CLARK, founder of Baby Einstein

"What I love about Nicole is that you don't need a dictionary to understand her advice. It's crystal clear, straight up, and spot-on."

—ALYSSA MILANO, actress and businesswoman

"Nicole delivers expert financial advice straight up, no chaser, in a tone that's as lively as it is likable."

—NEIL BLUMENTHAL AND DAVE GILBOA, founders of Warby Parker

"Nicole is the money expert with sensible advice to help you be the CEO of your own life."

—FRED DELUCA, Founder of Subway

"Essential reading for 21st century women wanting to rise to the top of the economic ladder."

—REBECCA TAYLOR, designer and cofounder of Rebecca Taylor

"Women are underrepresented among entrepreneurs. Nicole is a great guide to help us close that gap."

—DANIEL LUBETZKY, CEO and founder of KIND Snacks

"Nicole's books are fun and engaging and help you build your brand and rock your career."

—TONY HSEIH, CEO of Zappos

"Nicole brings to life in a highly readable way the real pitfalls and solutions of your career in a complex world."

—NIGEL TRAVIS, CEO and Chairman of Dunkin Brands

"Lapin's unfiltered, energetic advice speaks to anyone taking aim at their own career destiny."

—MIKE PERLIS, CEO of Forbes Media

"Nicole is truly inspiring and shares essential tips for women who want to take control of their lives."

—JOSIE NATORI, CEO and founder of The Natori Company

BECOMING
SUPER WOMAN

A Simple 12-Step Plan to Go from
Burnout to Balance

NICOLE LAPIN

BenBella Books, Inc.
10440 N. Central Expressway, Suite 800
Dallas, TX 75231
www.benbellabooks.com
Send feedback to feedback@benbellabooks.com

Printed in the United States of America
10 9 8 7 6 5 4 3 2 1

Library of Congress Control Number: 2019015074
9781946885937 (trade cloth)
9781948836678 (electronic)

Editing by Alexa Stevenson
Copyediting by Scott Calamar
Proofreading by Kimberly Broderick and Sarah Vostok
Text design and composition by Katie Hollister
Cover design by Sophia Chang
Cover photography by Nick Onken
Printed by Lake Book Manufacturing

Distributed to the trade by Two Rivers Distribution, an Ingram brand
www.tworiversdistribution.com

Special discounts for bulk sales are available.
Please contact bulkorders@benbellabooks.com.

To my former self,

who needed a hero, so that's what she became

And to all of you, my Super Women,

who have a hero inside of you, too

CONTENTS

Superwoman is the adversary of the women's movement.
—Gloria Steinem

INTRODUCTION

I wanted to be Superwoman for as long as I can remember. Do it all. Have it all. Be it all.

If you're like me, you probably looked up to some version of this character growing up—and most of us still do as grown-ass women. (Don't believe me? Take a look around the next costume party you go to.) I get it; Superwoman, after all, is pretty *and* pretty tough at the same time. Like, how *does* she maintain that bouncy blowout and look so smoking hot while also saving the world every day?!

But, for the longest time I never really stopped to think about *why* I aspired to be the embodiment of Superwoman. Have you? Or do you, a powerful, human woman, just idolize her because . . . you always have? Let's think about it for a second.

The Superwoman origin story goes, more or less, like this: Superman started saving the world. Then he saved Superwoman. And, then, Superwoman went on to save the world, multiple times—all while strutting in sassy red boots and remaining perfectly coiffed. So, it's basically a tale of a woman who was saved by a dude and then went right into saving everyone else. Never complaining. Never missing a beat. Is *that* truly who you want to be, what you want to strive for?

I don't. Her narrative is all about saving everyone else; in essence, dropping everything and even putting her own well-being in danger at the slightest suggestion that she is needed. Sure, she performs incredible feats, but *who* she is and how she *feels* is largely a mystery. In real life that plays out like this: Being all things to all people means you are nothing to yourself. And therein lies the *real* danger.

What I want to be is a *Super Woman*, not Superwoman. That space in between is important. That space allows me to define, on my own terms, what being "super" means for me and my goals without the pressure and limitations that come with the make-believe one-word version.

I'm betting your idolization of Superwoman is shifting as well, even if you're not fully aware of it yet. I can tell because the number-one question I get asked online or at the events is "Nicole, how can I stay happy and balanced and on top of my shit all the time like you?"

Well, I've never lied to my readers before, and I'm not going to do it now. I get that I might *look* or *seem* that way from what you know about me or my bio. You might know that I was the youngest anchor ever at CNN and hosted my own global show on CNBC in my midtwenties. You also might know that I found my niche after that delivering smart, no-nonsense advice about money and business to young women. And, you might know that I wrote two bestselling books (maybe you even read them!) on how to be a Rich Bitch and a Boss Bitch—someone who is in control of her financial life and her career future. All of this is true. But this is also true: I haven't always been balanced. I haven't been on top of my shit all the time. And, despite the success I've had, I haven't been consistently happy.

So while you know my bio, you probably don't know the whole story behind it. I had a broken and traumatic upbringing, one I hid from by working and then working some more. I reached the top of what I thought would be a long climb to success earlier than I'd ever imagined, becoming a network news anchor at just twenty-one. The more I achieved, the harder I worked. I thought that if I only worked harder, I would be even more successful—and *then* I would be happy. I told myself, "When I get to this network, I'll be happy." Then, I would get there and say, "Well, when I get this position, I'll be happy." But, breaking news: I wasn't. There was always another benchmark for success, always more to achieve, and always more realness to hide from.

Until very recently, if you had asked me to make a list of all the things I valued, it wouldn't have even occurred to me to put *myself* on it. The list was long with everything I'd always wanted: a super job, a super man, and an overall super life. But I wasn't devoting any time or effort into becoming a super woman first.

Until—also very recently—I had a breakdown. A complete and total mental, physical, and emotional breakdown. The developmental trauma I ignored or numbed with work for so many years finally kicked my ass. And only then did I have no choice but to make myself a priority.

Of course, I had experienced setbacks before, but my burnout and subsequent breakdown was the first and only time in my life that I fell down such a deep, dark hole that no one else could get me out of it. No one could swoop in to rescue me. I had to rescue myself.

That's when I realized: I'm *not* Superwoman—and I don't want to be. What I wanted to be was a Super Woman, a woman who, when she needed a hero, became one.

———————

My climb from rock bottom was a long one. If you're starting at a higher place than me, well, I'm not mad at ya. But you still have to climb to get to the top. There's no secret elevator. There's no quick fix. In fact, *there is no external solution to an internal problem.*

If you think you're okay just muscling through your problems as they arise or maybe even think you've "found" balance, keep thinking. Balance is not something you find, it's something you create, actively participate in, and practice all the time. And "not drowning" is not the same as "swimming." The space between "hanging in there" and being truly *happy* is where the real work is. My space was a pretty big one. But, if *I* could close that gap, then *anyone* can, including you.

While researching this book, I conducted the largest survey ever on women and burnout.* What I found wasn't particularly surprising, given how I felt myself, but it also wasn't good:

- 82 percent of respondents have experienced burnout—and 89 percent have felt they were on the verge of burnout.
- 49 percent have experienced a legitimate breakdown—and 71 percent have felt like they were close to experiencing one.

———————

* Developed with the help of the Institute for Applied Positive Research.

- 88 percent said there had been a time when mental or emotional stress affected their work.

- Almost 50 percent feel anxious four or more days a week.

- More than half (57 percent) said that their life did not feel balanced.

- 63 percent feel the pace of their life is sustainable.

Look at that last stat compared to what you read in the ones before it. How is it that so many of us are teetering on the edge of burnout or total breakdown—and yet the majority of us also feel that the pace of our lives is sustainable? What gives?! We are clearly *struggling*, but many of us are not yet ready to admit that it's a problem. I wasn't, until after I broke down. But until we face that reality head-on, we will continue to struggle and so will our careers, productivity, and well-being.

You might have seen headlines about how badass women from Hillary Clinton to Selena Gomez to YouTube superstar Lilly Singh (whose channel, ironically, is called "Superwoman") have run themselves into the ground. Here's what Sharon Osbourne said when she came back on her show after a public breakdown: "I was doing too much of everything, thinking 'I'm Superwoman, I'm so strong, I can handle this, I can handle that.'" But she wasn't Superwoman and neither was I—and neither were the 49 percent of women who said they'd had breakdowns, too.

Why is this happening to so many smart, successful, and strong women? The more I talk with other women—and I get that privilege all the time in my line of work—the more I realize how similar all our stories are. Here's what I'm hearing: We feel like we have to achieve more, be perfect, and power through whatever is going on. We are striving for balance in a fast-paced, hyperconnected world where we feel like we have to apologize if we take more than an hour to respond to an email. Working like crazy is driving us crazy. We are burning out.

Throughout my personal search for a way to get—and stay—better, I yearned for a playbook to tell me how to win the balance game without losing my career. Or myself. I didn't want some New Agey, holier-than-thou nonsense. I wanted a clear plan, broken down in a way I could understand and follow. But that didn't exist. So I went out and tried everything balance-related I could find, from equine therapy (yep, healing with horses) to extreme digital detox to floating meditation. I studied with spiritual healers, Eastern and Western medical practitioners, and even an astrologist. I went to Bali and on a silent retreat. I signed up for classes on quantum consciousness and behavioral theory. I tried treatments that retrain neuropathways and clear memories. I traveled the world and read everything I possibly could in search of answers.[*]

I gave myself a crash course in Emotional Wellness (more on that in the first step) and, as a result, ultimately found more success in my career than I ever did back when I was frantically responding to emails in the middle of the night. I found that nailing that was more beneficial than any business book I read or class I took. In this book, I'll lay out all the answers I arrived at, step-by-step—not as a guru or a scientific expert,

---

[*] If you want to read more about my adventures and the weird ways I researched this book/learned while learning to save myself, download the free e-book *The Super Woman Guide to Trips, Treatments, and Therapies for Balance (On a Budget)* at TheSuperWomanGuide.com. It gives you the exclusive knowledge and tricks that I learned from classes, experts, and healers all over the world—no wallet or passport required.

just as someone who fell hard and figured out how to get my ass back up.

Becoming Super Woman is a combination of my personal stories (the most personal yet) and actionable advice. It is laid out in the same way as my previous books: that is, in twelve steps, which I hope will make what has traditionally been seen as a fuzzy topic feel more manageable and the lessons more practical. As with my other books, you're welcome to follow the twelve steps in order, or to jump around "Choose Your Own Adventure" style. But I hope that you will read the book in its entirety in some fashion and then keep it so you can refer back to the sections you'll need at different times in your life. And I promise, life will let you know when you need a refresher.

Not sure where to start? Then Step 1: Killing Superwoman is the place for you. Be it stress, anxiety, an inability to say "no"—the list goes on—most of us face many different, intersecting "problems." In this step, we'll put a label on ours (which makes them less scary!) and then shift our thinking about them so we can stop hiding from them. Find yourself pulled in a million different directions by work projects, family obligations, and your social life? Check out Step 5: Boundaries, Bitch to learn how to set and maintain healthy boundaries (which will save your sanity *and* that of your loved ones). Are you overwhelmed by the daily grind . . . the growing assault of emails . . . the glowing screens? Head to Step 7: Put Down the F-ing Phone for a digital detox and to learn how being less plugged-in can actually make you more productive. Feeling super run-down, even though you just took a vacation? Look to Step 11: Check Yourself for more on identifying when you might need a mental health day, how to ask for one, and other tips for maintaining your Emotional Wellness even in the midst of chaos.

I used to think that being super meant excelling in everything: my career, my personal life, and, yeah, having a rockin' bod and the perfect outfit. But that ideal wasn't heroic at all. In fact, it was destructive. The pursuit of being perfectly put together made everything, well, fall apart.

The superpower I was missing was the ability to take care of myself. A *real* Super Woman—Super [space] Woman—is a woman who is dedicated to the pursuit of her own happiness, who decides what's important to her and makes time for it, who listens to what's going on in her own head and then deliberately and thoughtfully acts on it. A Super Woman is her own goddamn hero, who writes her own story and, when need be, saves herself.

Superwoman only exists in fiction. Super Women exist in real life. It's time to kill the idea that you have to be Superwoman. It's time to become a Super Woman.

STEP

1

KILLING SUPERWOMAN

One Woman's Problem Is Another Woman's Superpower

"**I**'m going to take your vitals and then take you to meet the team," the nurse said.

I had no idea where I was. The room had a generic wood dresser and desk that looked like something you'd see at summer camp. That is, if summer camp had been on the tenth floor of a building with windows that didn't open.

Before I could form a complete sentence, a blood pressure cuff was velcroed around my arm, and a thermometer was shoved under my tongue. I was in a hospital gown, and I had a laminated bracelet around my wrist.

"The team?" I asked in a crackly voice that didn't sound like my own.

"Your doctors will meet you down the hall with your social worker and your attending nurse."

"But *you're* a nurse," I said deliriously.

"I'm the morning nurse for everyone, but you'll have a designated nurse on your team."

I'd determined that I was in a hospital, but the bed I was in wasn't the big, bulky kind with plastic handrails. It was a normal bed, not quite Ikea quality, with a mattress that felt like cardboard and a super thin, itchy, mustard-colored blanket laid over an even thinner sheet.

"I'm going to walk you down the hall," said the nurse, prodding me up.

I was so tired. All I wanted to do was sleep—in that crappy bed, on the floor, anywhere.

My eyes were sore and barely open as I walked down the long hallway, lit by blinding fluorescent lights that felt like they might swallow me up. The nurse guided me into what looked like a sterile white classroom, with four chairs arranged in a row like a panel and another chair facing them. I guessed I was supposed to sit in that one, as the four across from it were already occupied by four people with clipboards. They were in normal clothes, and I was in a hospital gown and pink socks with little white treads on the bottom. I've walked into some intimidating rooms in my life—boardrooms at Wall Street banks, greenrooms at major TV networks—but none more intimidating than this.

"Hi, Nicole," said the man in the first chair from behind his clipboard.

"Hi."

"Do you know why you are here?"

"No." But, as I said it, I realized I *did* know why I was there. I looked down at my hands. They were trembling uncontrollably.

I was in the psych ward.

"Actually, yes," I said.

"And why are you here?" the man asked in a monotone.

Then came the longest pause. They were waiting for me to answer. And I couldn't. I couldn't believe how I had gotten to this place.

Oh. My. God, I thought. *I'm never going to get out of here.*

"I am here because . . . because . . ." I started to cry. I couldn't finish the sentence. I could only cry and say "because" over and over.

I couldn't say anything else because I didn't yet believe the words that were to follow. From what I could remember, I had been admitted to the emergency room around midnight after police picked me up on a street corner. I'd had nothing in my stomach for days except alcohol and coffee. I had no cell phone. No money. No keys. No ID. Just cigarettes in my pocket, even though I don't smoke, along with matches (because to this day I don't know how to use a lighter). And a full bottle of Ambien.

"Do you remember what brought you here last night?"

"S . . . I," I said slowly, remembering the clinical term I'd heard throughout the night before. I had probably talked to ten doctors, nurses, and EMTs between midnight and 4 AM when I'd been taken to my camp-style bedroom. "SI" stands for "suicidal ideation." Somehow it felt less embarrassing to say the acronym instead of the actual term.

"And why did you plan to kill yourself last night by taking an entire bottle of sleeping pills?" the same guy asked. The other three scribbled notes without looking at me.

At that moment I knew I needed to dig deep, rising above what felt like the worst experience of my life, to show these people that I was okay now and healthy enough to go home. (Even though deep down I knew I wasn't.)

"I was really sad and really stressed," I said steadily. "I wasn't taking care of myself and I slipped. I'm sorry, is it possible to have my clothes back?"

They looked at me like I was a zoo animal.

"Not yet," the man said. "We need to monitor you for a while."

"What's 'a while'?" I asked, trying hard to sound calm and composed even though I was shivering. I was shivering partly because I was freezing but mostly because I was scared.

"We'll keep checking in with you, and then make a determination. Do you have any suicidal thoughts right now?"

"No."

It was true. All my thoughts were focused on trying to communicate with my usual poise, charisma, and energy so they'd see that I didn't *need* to be there. But I couldn't find *that* Nicole. It wasn't just that I didn't feel like my usual self; I felt like a stranger in my own body. I wanted to yell for someone to help me, but I knew the only people who could hear me had a totally different idea of what helping me meant.

In the three days that followed, I went from despondent and depressed to humbled. I hate when actors say they are "humbled" when they win an Oscar. Um, that's not "humbling," that's fucking amazing. Spend some time in the psych ward with a whole different cast of characters, and then you'll *really* feel humbled.

At first, I was that girl sitting in the corner, drinking black coffee by herself. There was no phone or internet; I didn't remember any of my friends' numbers so I couldn't make calls from the communal landline in the cafeteria. Even if I had remembered anyone's number, I didn't know how to explain what had happened yet. I was alone and acted like a loner.

Slowly, I began talking to others and signing up for the group classes, like horticulture and music therapy. I started treating it like the camp I never went to. My fellow "campers" ranged from a musical theater star to an eighty-year-old orthodox Jewish man. There were no padded rooms or screaming in the middle of the night, just a bunch of people who were suffering like me and needed to get better . . . as one does in a hospital. There were homeless people and there were CEOs, patients from all walks of life. I came to appreciate the psych ward as a great equalizer, like the subway or the flu.

The day I was discharged, I walked right outside onto First Avenue in New York City, holding a plastic bag of my belongings. No one was there waiting for me, and I didn't have my phone when I checked in, so I couldn't call anyone. I didn't really want anyone to see me like that, anyway.

I was alone. But at that point I didn't feel lonely anymore. I knew the journey to come would be largely a solo one, so I might as well get down with that on Day 1.

I walked all the way home. It was a few solid miles, but I felt like I could have walked outside forever, more appreciative of being outside, walking, that day than any other. I had no phone to look at like I usually would have, so instead I looked around at the city, grateful for every little thing I saw. I looked at the people I passed like I never had before when I'd walked with my face staring at a screen or my mind obsessing over my to-do list. They had no idea where I'd just come from, and I had no idea whether they might have been there once, too.

SUPER WOMAN, INTERRUPTED

"But you seem so put together!" you might think after reading my story. I know, I've heard it a million times.

The thing about feeling crappy on the inside is that you can *look* totally "put together" on the outside. You can't see the emotional wounds someone might be carrying like you can physical scrapes or scars. Often, we see someone who looks like a kick-ass warrior on the outside and have no idea of the inner war she has fought—or is still fighting.

I thought I was Superwoman. I'd wrapped up shooting for the second season of my TV show and had just finished touring the country promoting my second book. I was a badass *New York Times* bestselling author who preached badassery to other women. I was, from all outward appearances, at the height of my career. The top of the world.

And then, I fell.

Trying to be Superwoman nearly killed me. So, I needed to kill the idea of her to save myself. I set out to become a Super Woman, a woman who takes care of the inside as much as or more than the outside, a woman who *feels* as "put together" as she looks.

YOU HAVE A PROBLEM

The first step to becoming a Super Woman is admitting you aren't Superwoman, like I eventually did. Embracing it, even. We all have problems. And it doesn't matter if your problem is feeling depressed or an occasional case of sleep deprivation—if it's causing you distress, then it's serious, and it's time to get serious about taking care of it.

"Wait a minute, Lapin," I hear you saying, "my problems aren't anywhere near the *Girl, Interrupted* level of yours! I'm a little stressed, but basically fine!" Well, guess what? If you don't take care of yourself, you still run the risk of breaking down like I did, burning out, or at the very least, falling short of the life you want and deserve (and that outcome should be unacceptable to you, too). We all have something going on that threatens to knock us off-balance. So, what's your "something"?

CONFESSIONS
OF A SUPER WOMAN

I'll Go First

My "something" is that I have struggled with post-traumatic stress disorder (PTSD).

I didn't even know that's what it was called until after my breakdown. I met with tons of doctors and specialists and even did an outpatient psychiatric program. I took my recovery seriously and shined a light on some of the deepest, darkest places in me. They weren't fun places to go, but the trip there was long overdue.

I was always focused on where I was going, so I never truly confronted where I had been, which was a chronically abusive, violent, and unstable upbringing that played out in real time like a Lifetime movie. My mother kidnapped me when I was three years old and changed my name while she was undergoing a nasty divorce from my father. She was arrested and granted monitored visitation with me while I lived with my father—a brilliant surgeon who invented new ways of performing surgery with limited blood loss. He was also an alcoholic and drug addict who hung around a revolving crew of drug dealers, hookers, and criminals. There wasn't a week that went by that police or social workers weren't called to my house, nor was there one that he didn't save a patient's life. The dichotomy of public success and private struggle is branded into my DNA. He ultimately died of an overdose when I was eleven. Until then, their sordid divorce—fraught with allegations of molestation, rape, and arson—was all over the papers for years and one quote from the *Los Angeles Times* asserted "neither Lapin is fit to be a parent."

For a long time, I hid from my traumatic childhood by self-medicating—not with drugs, but with work. The more I worked, the more I felt like I was okay and stronger than the trauma. But it was only a matter of time until I couldn't outwork it anymore. My breakdown wasn't so much a spontaneous combustion precipitated by a single event as a lifetime of smoldering embers finally catching fire—and incinerating everything in their path.

If you've ever thought personal stuff has nothing to do with work—whether it's a mental health issue, an eating disorder, relationship drama, or plain-old everyday stress—you've thought wrong. In the end, what do *you* think was more detrimental to my career: not responding to every single email within an hour or having to bail on obligations and cancel projects because I was in the damn psych ward? Exactly.

To be clear, the psych ward sucked. It really fucking sucked. But it was also one of the most rewarding places I've ever been, because going there forced me to get serious about taking care of myself for the first time.

I used to pretend like my trauma didn't exist so that it wouldn't get in the way of my success. I was certain that it would be the kryptonite that would eventually bring me down. But just as I was killing the idea that I was Superwoman, so, too, did I kill the idea that my biggest problem was my biggest weakness.

SO, WHAT'S YOUR PROBLEM?!

Before you can unlock the power of your problems, you have to know what they are. Give them a name and you take away some of their power over you. Are you not feeling like yourself? Are you feeling far from . . . super? How so? Be specific.

If you're like the women I surveyed who feel like they are on the verge of a breakdown, you might be experiencing burnout-like symptoms. Burnout often coexists with or acts as a "gateway" for other, clinical conditions, namely depression and anxiety.*

---

* While burnout has been studied and treated as a clinical condition by psychologists for years, it was officially recognized by the World Health Organization just as this book was going to print. The WHO added it to the International Classification of Diseases alongside other mental health issues—a big deal when it comes to diagnosis and insurance coverage.

- **Burnout** is a state of physical, mental, or emotional exhaustion—when the demands of your job or life in general have become so overwhelming that you don't feel like you can cope. It's often caused by extended stress but feels like its opposite. Instead of feeling "up," you feel empty and unmotivated. A quick way to tell if you've ventured into burnout territory is by noticing how you feel after you go on vacation: Do you feel reenergized and recharged after returning to work? If so, you just needed a little time to step away and rest. But if you still feel exhausted, cynical, and inefficient within days (or even sooner) after your return, you may be experiencing burnout.

- **Depression** is a feeling of helplessness and hope-lessness. Some people feel sad and tired if they are depressed, while some feel on edge and can't sleep, and others just feel flat or numb. One common sign of depression is being unable to enjoy the things you usually like to do. Depression can be situational, like after a bad breakup or a death in the family, or it can be a chronic issue (as in you feel shitty even when things are good).

- **Anxiety** is a strong sense of worry, nervousness, or unease. You might feel jittery and emotional, or have physical symptoms like nausea or headaches. Anxiety can also be situational, and it's totally normal to feel anxious about an upcoming event, like a big presentation or a medical procedure, especially if the outcome is uncertain. But if you're feeling anxious nearly all the time, whether there's a big project looming or not, you might have an anxiety disorder. Anxiety disorders are the most common mental health issues, affecting almost one in five adults, and the prevalence among women is roughly 2.5 times greater than among men.

We tend to use these terms interchangeably. But the words you use matter, especially when you are describing yourself—and especially when you are seeking help, whether by tackling the problem yourself or by getting support from your community or a medical professional. A broken bone shows up on an X-ray, but only you (and your psychiatrist) can tell when something is wrong with what you are feeling inside.

Everyone experiences situational anxiety or feels depressed from time to time, but not everyone suffers from the clinical disorders of anxiety or depression. Sometimes these are referred to, and feel like, "capital-A anxiety" and "capital-D depression" (even though both the situational and clinical kinds of anxiety and depression are technically capitalized the same way). Figuring out whether the problem you are experiencing is a clinical one is something a professional can help you with.

FYI

I know that you are more than a label and so am I. But labeling my problems has allowed me to reframe them in a way that works for me. The label has been a jumping-off point for me to change their narrative and connotation in my life.

Your problems are nothing to hide or be embarrassed about. Nor do they make you weak. Quite the contrary. Your power lies in the fact that no one else is you. And, by "you," I mean *all* of you.

After my breakdown, I finally confronted my PTSD diagnosis and all of the symptoms—good and bad—that came along with it. The truth is, I wouldn't be who I am today without dealing with the depressive episodes or times of hypervigilance and arousal (not the sexy kind) that came from the diagnosis. Without them, I probably wouldn't have worked so hard and might never have had the opportunities I received as a result, including being able to write this book for you now. And if that part of me is what got me to where I am now, then I have to consider the possibility that it might just be the last thing I ever expected it to be: a superpower.

My mission was to find the power in facing my problems, not to change myself or be problem free (problems are a game of whack-a-mole anyway: as soon as you tackle one, another pops up for you to attack). You can do the same thing. Lots of the issues and personality traits we view as holding us back can also push us forward.

Take a problem we've all had: stress. I don't need to get all clinical on you here because I'm pretty sure you've been in (and might even currently be experiencing) a state of stress, where your emotions and adrenaline are in overdrive. We tend to think of stress as bad, and it definitely can be, like if you're stressed because your boss is yelling at you or you're worried about making rent. But, physiologically, stress is neutral. What makes it positive or negative is how you respond to it. Just like there is "good" fat (like avocados) or debt (student loans) and "bad" fat (like fried food) or debt (credit card debt), there is good and bad stress. There is actually a word for good stress: "eustress." It's what makes working on a big-deal project you are passionate about so exciting. You can't get rid of all stress, and you wouldn't want to. Life without stress would be pretty boring. Plus, you wouldn't want Tom Brady to block out his eustress during a big game and be super mellow, right? No. (Unless you're not a Patriots fan.)

And because you're the quarterback of your own life, it's up to you how you play a "problem" like stress, or perfectionism, or sensitivity. It can drive you down the field or it can make you fumble. So, what's the call gonna be, QB?

SOMETIMES PROBLEMS ARE SUPERPOWERS BY ANOTHER NAME

Our brains have a "negativity bias" that predisposes us to focus on and feel the bad more than the good. This may have been helpful when we were cavewomen, but it's up to us Super Women to actively reframe the default negative and rewire "problems" positively:

PROBLEM		SUPERPOWER
I'm a pessimist	→	I'm realistic and prepared in a crisis

Pessimism is certainly zero fun for other people to be around. But using pessimism defensively, to set yourself up to beat low expectations, can be a powerful approach—better than being too optimistic and then missing the mark. What's more, those with a cautious outlook are often less flustered when things go wrong.

I'm super sensitive	→	I'm empathetic and perceptive

A sensitive person (like yours truly!) often crumbles in the face of criticism. But, your sensitivity can also be a powerful business tool: Your awareness of other people's feelings can help you finesse tricky conversations and make you a persuasive leader. Being hyperperceptive can also help you understand people and situations better than others can, giving you an advantage when working out the best approach.

I'm a worrier	→	I'm always thinking a step ahead

Intense worry can be crippling. But you can use a lesser tendency toward fretting to your advantage by being organized, careful, and on top of deadlines. Your worrier's habit of asking "What if?" makes you the queen of contingency plans and lets you foresee potential pitfalls—and avoid them.

I'm a perfectionist	→	I notice details other people miss

The need to make every little thing perfect, if it goes unchecked, can make it impossible to be productive. But that same knack for meticulousness can be an asset in any number of professions, giving you an eye for detail and ensuring that you're never embarrassed by a sloppy error.

I'm easily distrac—Look! A squirrel!	→	I'm a creative multitasker

An ADHD diagnosis or other problems focusing might require medication or adjustments to your workplace setting. But having a brain that tends to leap from one tangent to another lets you see connections others might not. And harnessing the power of your creative mind in organized, preplanned twenty- or thirty-minute intervals could make you a masterful multitasker.

I have problems; you have problems; we all have problems. The point is, the only problem that truly is career kryptonite is the problem of ignoring your problems. So look those babies right in the eye, give them a wink, and make them your new best friends. A mental health professional once put it to me this way: If oysters can take the sand that creeps into their shells and turn that into something as beautiful and valuable as a pearl, then so can we.

PROBLEM-SOLVING 101

We learn how to solve for the angle of a triangle or the speed of a train in school, but we don't learn the skills we need to deal with our personal problems and take care of ourselves, which will get us a lot farther in life than the Pythagorean theorem ever will. Once I taught myself personal finance, I thought that it was the number-one thing I would have kids learn if I were in charge of the world. That's until I learned about the importance of a set of behaviors and qualities I call "Emotional Wellness."

Let's run a quick equation:

$$Emotional\ intelligence + Mental\ wellness$$
$$= Emotional\ Wellness$$

where *emotional intelligence* is your capacity to be aware of, control, and express your feelings and manage relationships, and *mental wellness* is your mental, social, and emotional health.

You've likely heard of *emotional intelligence,* or EQ, and its effect on getting ahead in your career. It is connected to both better workplace performance and higher salary. People with high EQ excel at perceiving, understanding, using, and managing emotions. Studies show that when people have roughly equal IQ and skill, EQ accounts for 90 percent of what makes some of those people more successful than others.

You also likely know that *mental wellness* is a state of psychological health and well-being. People who take care of their mental wellness are able to sustain a baseline of contentment while creating and maintaining healthy relationships. They also have the ability to cope with the demands of everyday life, and are resilient when shit happens.

High EQ and stellar mental wellness are each important on their own. But to be the most successful Super Woman you can be, you really need both. And they need each other. For instance, emotional intelligence gives you the ability to recognize that your emotions are heading downhill before they get out of control, while mental wellness makes it easier to access that awareness and gives you the resources to act on it. The stronger each of these pieces are, the stronger your resulting Emotional Wellness will be (just like how when you add two big numbers together, you get an even bigger one).

To use finance terminology, Emotional Wellness can be your greatest asset or your greatest liability—especially when it comes to your career. In other words, having it can foster your success and lacking it can destroy it. It's what welcomes balance and wards off burnout.

MAYBE SHE'S BORN WITH IT (BUT PROBABLY NOT)

We are not born knowing how to cultivate Emotional Wellness or how to use it to crush life. These things are learned. Yes, changing the IQ you were born with is hard, but upping your EQ and mental wellness is *absolutely* doable.

I did it. And I'm going to share everything I've discovered—through research, and a lot of trial and error—along the way. But mastering and maintaining your Emotional Wellness is up to you.

I'm not gonna lie—it's work. Every. Single. Day. But I can tell you this: Even though it's basically free, this knowledge is worth more to your success than anything you'll learn in grad school or any of the countless professional seminars on getting ahead you might take. Yet we often ignore these skills entirely in professional development. Instead, we take out hefty student loans, study, and network our booties off, even though those efforts don't correlate directly to success like working on your Emotional Wellness does. This book is a crash course in the most important subject that none of us learned in school.

But let me be super clear before we do this: I am not a shrink. I am not a scientist. I have no formal training in the brain or mental health. I wasn't sure I would ever become mentally healthy myself, much less be in a position to *teach* anyone how to do it. You might be thinking: then why *are* you teaching this—you're not an expert!?!

Believe me, you're not thinking anything I haven't thought myself. I've had many long conversations with myself about whether or not I had any business writing this book. When I quieted the mean girl inside my head, though, I realized that I'm *exactly* the person who should be writing about Emotional Wellness. I'm not an expert in self-care and self-love just yet, and I'll never claim to be, but I *am* an expert (or as close as you can get) in self-harm and self-hate, and having worked my way from the latter concepts to the former makes me the perfect guide for anyone trying to do the same. I understand how precious Emotional Wellness is because I know what it is like not to have it, and for me, figuring out how to develop it, and then maintain it, wasn't just some academic interest—it was a necessity. My expertise is my experience: living it and making it through—not just in one piece, but stronger than ever.

––––––––––––––

After finishing the otherworldly walk home to my apartment from the hospital, one of the first things I did was cut off my white hospital bracelet with a huge sigh of relief and gratitude. Relief for coming through that experience, and gratitude for the chance to get on a healthier path. As the bracelet came off, I was surprised to see another band underneath it that I hadn't even realized was there. This one was yellow, and all it said was "Fall Risk." I've since Googled it and learned that everyone gets a "Fall Risk" band in the psych ward because, unlike patients in other parts of the hospital, most psych patients are allowed to walk around freely within the ward; changes in medications, however, put them at greater risk for falling. Those two simple words—"Fall Risk"—would go on to become a phrase that had great meaning for me.

I keep that yellow band in a frame on my desk as a daily reminder that without the right care and maintenance, I am a "Fall Risk." Not physically, but mentally. Of course, I'm going to do everything I can not to slip again—by harnessing the power I've developed as a real-life Super Woman. And by the end of this book, you'll have that power, too.

BOTTOM LINE*

Conventional Wisdom: Having a breakdown means that I'm weak.

Having a breakdown is not fun. I've been there. And BTW, tons of high-powered people I know have, too (and you're gonna hear from some of them throughout this book). It doesn't mean you're weak. The best way to avoid another breakdown in the future is a combination of compassion and tough love. First, give your former self empathy for what she didn't know. Then, learn that. Grow. And don't go back.

Conventional Wisdom: Problems are bad.

The way you view and talk about your problems can make all the difference. Unlocking their power requires that you first identify them. Then, reframe and manage them. It means harnessing the good while recognizing what is difficult for you and where you might need support. Often the only thing standing between distress and success is asking for help. And in order to do that, you have to identify just what it is you need help with in the first place.

---

* PS—Because this book focuses on how prioritizing yourself will make you more successful, I want to debunk some conventional wisdom about Emotional Wellness and your career. I include a "Bottom Line" at the end of every step in my books because a) a little review never hurt anyone; b) it's a finance term (swoon!) that just means how much you or a company is making when all is said and done—always important information to have; and, c) the best success strategies are ones that come from unconventional thinking. After all, "self-care" is not just a buzzword or a luxury, it is a tool for achieving more success than you ever imagined. While it's all too easy to put yourself at the bottom of your to-do list, your bottom line takes a hard hit when you do.

Conventional Wisdom: If I just work harder, I'll get ahead.

It's easy to de-prioritize yourself in favor of working harder. But not taking care of yourself is not helping you get ahead; it's holding you back.

STEP

2

"SELF" IS MY FAVORITE FOUR-LETTER WORD

Behind Every Successful Woman Is Herself

Like a lot of angsty young adults, I was obsessed with the Coldplay song "Fix You":

> *Lights will guide you home*
> *And ignite your bones*
> *And I will try to fix you*

I would play it on repeat—as one does with song obsessions—and yearn for someone to "fix" me. Even now, sans angst, I still love the song . . . but I hate the line. Lights may guide you home, but you're not fixing anyone, and ain't no one fixing you.

In Step 1, you admitted you aren't Superwoman. Now, it's time to become a Super Woman. The first thing you need to do to be one: commit to yourself. Fall in love with yourself and your life—not because you or it is perfect, but because it's you and yours—instead of with some fictitious and unattainable ideal.

It's easy to keep going back to clichéd phrases like "fix you" and "you complete me" because you've heard them for so long: from song lyrics, friends, and exes. Well, spoiler alert, your life isn't going to play out like *Jerry Maguire*. In this step, I'm going to remind you that you never needed fixing in the first place, then explain how to tap into the best parts of yourself and show you how to complete *you*.

PUT A RING ON IT

A lot of women set out to "date" themselves, but I wanted more than the cursory dinner and a movie. (Although, if you haven't taken yourself to dinner and a movie alone, I suggest you do so ASAP. It's awesome.) I wanted to be exclusive. For me, "dating myself" meant going all the way, being all in.

CONFESSIONS
OF A SUPER WOMAN

The Day I Got Engaged

"Do you have that in a size five and a half?" I asked the saleswoman at Tiffany's who was hovering around, waiting for me to request help.

"Of course, madam," she said as she put on her white gloves.

I slipped the ring she had pulled from the case onto my ring finger and extended my arm to see how it looked from a distance.

"It's very pretty," she said (which, of course, is what she would say even if it wasn't).

"Yes, it is . . . Can I try on a few different styles to see which one fits best with the rest of my jewelry? Because, you know, I'm going to be wearing it every day."

"Of course, madam. You know, a lot of women come in to see what they like, and then have a friend 'suggest' it when the guy asks for help picking out a ring," said the saleswoman coyly. I might have even seen her wink.

I just smiled and looked at the options on the velvet tray she placed on the counter in front of me.

"You know, girls have to stick together, and it's the best way to guarantee you get what you want," she said.

"I'll take that one," I said, pointing to a delicate silver band with a small but mighty diamond baguette tucked into the middle of it.

There was an awkward pause, then a (very formal) gasp as she expressed her embarrassment. "Oh, madam! I'm so sorry, I thought you were getting engaged."

"I am," I said with a big smile, hoping it would be contagious. "I'll take it in one of those blue boxes, please."

Like a lot of young girls, I fantasized about the day I would get engaged. My fantasies didn't include much about the specifics of the event, but they all involved a ring in a little blue box. That is, a Tiffany box (probably the only fancy jewelry maker I knew).

For a long time, I thought I would wait to go on vacations and have adventures until I found someone I was serious about. So, I waited. And waited. And I didn't go on vacations, and I didn't have adventures. Then I was done waiting.

All my younger self wanted was to get engaged—and to have a blue box involved. She didn't stipulate that there was a guy on the other side of that box, and over time I came to realize that there didn't need to be. So, I filled in the details, and bought my own damn ring in my own blue Tiffany box. I got serious . . . about myself.

I think a lot about my younger self. I feel a responsibility to help her fulfill her dreams. And I'm not going to let her down.

Right-handed rings date back to the days of prohibition, symbolizing women's earning power and independence. They were popularized in the mid-1900s by actresses Elizabeth Taylor and Natalie Wood and have come to mean a commitment to yourself, regardless of if you have or want a ring on the other hand or not.

I'm guessing that you value commitment. That's good, because you can't divorce yourself. There's literally no one else with you through everything "'til death do you part." So love yourself first; it's who you will be undoubtedly spending the rest of your life with.

ARE YOU INTO YOURSELF?

Being a Super Woman means taking care of yourself. But it's hard to take care of someone you don't know, or worse, don't like. So let's get to know ourselves, and start not just liking but falling madly in love with that girl.

In the back of my notebook (yes, I carry around an actual spiral-bound notebook everywhere I go, like Linus carries his blanket), I have a few evergreen lists. These are my "Super Woman cheat sheets," lists I refer to when I'm feeling like a "Fall Risk." The first one is affectionately titled "How I Am Awesome." It reminds me *why* I put a ring on it. Here are some of my highlights:

- I am a great gift giver.
- I am a fighter.
- I have sweet writing skills.
- I can give a speech without notes.
- I can recite many of Shakespeare's sonnets and Tupac's songs by heart.
- I am great at researching adventures and then actually taking them.
- I can change clothes in a Lyft without the driver seeing anything.
- I can have fun talking to anyone, from a CEO, to a kid, to a farmer.

Throughout the book I'll go first with the hard exercises and "show you mine" in hopes that it's easier for you to show me (or yourself) yours. So, your turn. How are *you* awesome? List all of the ways. Don't edit, at least not at first. They can be anything: from winning a Pulitzer to having sick origami skills to being able to say the alphabet backward.

When you're done making your list, go back and look for ways to tweak those attributes into the most positive and powerful version possible. If you wrote, "I don't interrupt others when talking," well, that definitely is awesome, but maybe it would be even better as "I'm great at listening and having productive conversations." If you "don't fall down on black diamond runs on the ski slope," then you are a) badass and b) "a skilled skier who has mastered the most advanced ski runs," which is what you should write down. Even if it seems like a good thing "not" to do something, rephrasing to focus on the thing you *do* versus what you *don't* will make the already awesome even more so. If you're still feeling stuck, start small ("I have excellent handwriting") and then widen your scope ("I am a strong writer who can articulate my ideas").

Who's the Awesomest of Them All?

If you're having a hard time liking who you see in the mirror on the wall, think about yourself on your hypothetical "best day." Look at that day like you are watching a scene in a movie. Who is that woman? What is she doing? What does she look like? What is she wearing? Where does she live? Who is she with? How does she feel around those people? How do you think they feel about her?

Describe everything like you would if you

> were casting a movie of your own life (I'm hop-
> ing for Mila Kunis in mine). What would that
> actress need to know to embody that woman?
> Sometimes seeing yourself in the third person
> is all you need to notice the things that make
> you awesome that everyone else already sees.

Does this exercise make you squirm? Like you're embarrassed to be "bragging" about yourself? Get over it. You wouldn't
hesitate to gush over the good stuff about your partner or best
friend; you should be just as generous describing yourself.

Your list might only have one item on it to start with, but
keep adding to it when you think of other things (and you will).
Keeping a list of what makes you great will train your mind
to stay on the lookout for them. Think of it as a love letter
to yourself, from yourself, that you look at when you need a
little . . . well, love.

What happens when you start recognizing these things
about yourself is that you realize how completely awesome you
already are. Without anyone else. Without fixing. And yes, I
could tell you that. Friends or your mom could tell you that.
But what matters is that *you* know it.

LIVE YOUR BEST SOLO LIFE

Let's add "finding yourself" to our list of clichéd phrases that
suck. That phrase assumes, of course, that you are lost in the
first place, which you are not. So before you set out to hike the
Appalachian Trail in an effort to "find yourself," remember that
it's actually impossible to lose yourself, even though it might

not always feel that way. You're stuck with yourself, sister, for better and for worse. So get used to it, and get down with it.

BE SELFISH

If someone calls us "selfish," it feels like a diss. Why? Because our society has told us that it is; like being overly focused on yourself is a *bad* thing, especially for a woman. But the actual definition of "selfish" is "concerned chiefly with one's own personal profit or pleasure." Well now *that* sounds like a compliment, right?

And you know what actually should be a diss, and isn't? Being called "self*less*." This is often used as a compliment, especially for a woman. But the definition of "selfless" is "having no concern for oneself." That doesn't sound like something anyone should aspire to. Even if your goal is to help others, you're probably able to contribute most when you're also well cared for yourself—aka, selfish.

Being "selfish" is only bad if you're hurting others. Let's agree to 1) not hurt others, k?, 2) embrace the idea that putting your needs first is the best and healthiest thing you can do, and 3) remember that "self" is a four-letter word . . . and we love our four-letter words. So, the next time someone calls you "selfish," say "thank you." And if they call you "selfless," offer a polite correction—and remind them who's looking out for number one.

POP QUIZ

Picking up this book was a good step toward taking care of yourself, but what else have you done for you lately? *Just* for you?

1. **You want to see a particular movie, but no one you know wants to go. You:**
    a) Go see the movie, solo.
    b) Ask around until you find someone who will see it with you.
    c) Wait for it to come out on Netflix.
2. **When you're asked to name your hobbies, you say:**
    a) "Lately I'm super into [insert random cool class you're taking, activity you're passionate about, etc.]."
    b) "Spending time with friends and family."
    c) "Working."
3. **When asked to rank your top three priorities, you list:**
    a) Myself, family, work
    b) Family, work, myself
    c) Work, work, work

If you answered mostly As, you have the right Super Woman mentality going.

If you answered mostly Bs, you need to keep a close eye on the ring you put on yourself.

> If you answered mostly Cs, revisit your "How I
> Am Awesome" list as many times as it takes to want
> to hang out with that woman some more.

If you're so immersed with your job or other people that your needs get ignored, you should realize that they don't say "put your oxygen mask on first before helping others" on the plane just to fill time before takeoff. You're not going to be any help to anyone else if you are crashing and burning.

Getting comfortable doing things for and with yourself is a key part of being a Super Woman. Sure, it can be easy to find yourself completely absorbed in a role (a new job, motherhood) or a romantic relationship. We've all been *there*. His friends. His schedule. All your time and energy, all day, every day. But according to multiple large-scale studies (and an unofficial survey of my happy couple friends) having a fulfilling life outside of the relationship is the key to a healthy, long-lasting partnership. When you have your own stuff going on, you ensure that if you lose something, like a guy or a job, you don't feel "lost." You still have your already-super life and your already-super self. Any addition only makes it *more* super.

And while we are at it, let's ditch another BS cliché: referring to someone or something as "my everything," "my other half," or, worse, "my better half." Ew. No one on this earth is another half of you—they are just another planet in your orbit. And no one and no thing can be your sunshine when you are the damn sun.

DON'T WAIT FOR THE LIGHT AT THE END OF THE TUNNEL

. . . light that bitch up yourself.

I'll let you in on a little secret: Whenever I make a wish—on a penny, an eyelash, in a tunnel, or at 11:11 PM—I always wish for happiness. "I want to be happy," I've said to myself as I closed my eyes and made my wish, for as long as I can remember. I feel like I can share that with you and still have my wish come true, because I'm a pretty happy bitch now.

I'm sure there are millions of pennies in wishing wells across the globe with the same wish attached to them. A lot of this book focuses on how you can make that wish come true for yourself—and it won't even cost you that penny. In fact, it's free: you just have to stop wishing and start participating relentlessly in making it happen.

Does this sound familiar? "When I get *there*, I will be happy." And when you get "there," it goes like this: "Well, now when I just get *there*, I will *really* be happy." The "if I just work harder," "if I'm just more successful," "if I just lose five pounds," ". . . *then* I'll be happy" promise was one I made to myself all the time during the first fifteen years of my career.

The problem was this: There is always another "there" to strive for. You work hard and get a raise, and then it's "Well, now shouldn't I take on a higher position?" Or you lose those five pounds, only to say, "Well, what's five pounds when it could be ten?" Is it *ever* enough?

Well, it is now, if you decide it is. Enough with the "not being enough" stuff already. This doesn't mean letting go of your ambition; it means taking the time to appreciate how much you already have. Studies have shown that increased levels of happiness *lead* to success, not the other way around. For years I had the equation backward. If you can raise your levels of optimism and deepen your social connections with others, every single performance indicator improves dramatically. You can increase your success rates for the rest of your life and your happiness levels will flatline, but if you raise your level of happiness, your success rate will only slope higher and higher.

When I start to slip into old thought patterns of "I'll be happy when . . ." and feel impossibly far from loving my life, or "having it all" (you'll hear more about my feelings on that phrase in the next step), I flip the phrase to "It makes me happy that . . ." and think about what I *do* have:

- Friends who will always be there for me if I need them; if shit hits the fan, I know they will take me in as family
- An apartment with furniture that I'm obsessed with
- A network of strong professional contacts I've kept up with over the years
- Three published books
- The best coffee maker on the planet (which fuels keeping up with all the above)

It's natural to focus on the bad or annoying things going on in your life; these things tend to stress us out, which is a very physical reaction and one that's difficult to ignore. But feeding them with constant attention and rumination only allows them to grow. Of course, there will always be a "worst-case scenario" and some bad stuff; that's life. But there's also always a "best-case scenario" and some good stuff, probably more than you realize during stressful moments, good stuff that's likely starved for your attention.

Harvard Health studies have shown that gratitude in particular contributes significantly to your happiness, which makes you more productive and more successful (plus, according to Harvard grad Elle Woods, "happy people don't kill other people"). Just think about the word "appreciation." It means two things: increasing in value over time and giving thanks. So you want to appreciate? Then appreciate.

Go for the Gratitude Gold

A simple journaling exercise every morning and night can help you ditch any self-hating thoughts you might have. Neuroscientists have found that practicing gratitude makes your brain happy (boosts dopamine and serotonin levels) and creates positive feedback loops. Even if you feel like you have nothing to be grateful for, the act of just searching for something to be grateful for can have positive effects. Don't overthink it. It's not some elaborate ceremony. I practice gratitude for five minutes twice a day by filling in the following five prompts:

Three Things I'm Grateful for Today
- The smell of coffee
- My orchid that is still kicking
- A fluffy comforter and clean sheets

Three Things I'm Excited About Today
- Going to boxing class
- Meeting with a producing partner
- Researching weekend plans

Three People I'm Grateful for Today
- My doorman Julio
- My agent Jared
- My social media and website wizard-resses Megan and Sabrina (okay that makes four)

One Mantra I Want to Remember Today
- I am a work in progress and a master-piece at the same time.

One Thing I Will Do to Be of Service Today
(Note: interpret this however you want, you just have to be doing something or "serving" someone else)
- I will call my friend Kristy because she needs a little extra TLC after a breakup.

For the nighttime entry, try to think about specific moments or actions so you don't end up repeating answers like "my family" every day. So instead of writing that you're grateful for "my daughter," perhaps you write that you are grateful for "the hug I gave my daughter when she got home from school." Not only does the nuance help you stick to the practice, but it helps you notice, be present for, and savor positive moments throughout your day. (BTW: positive memories form only if you are present in the emotion of them for ten to fifteen seconds.)

You can use this template, make your own, or pick up *The Super Woman Journal* (shameless plug), which has prompts similar to this to help you feel balanced on the regular. You can write them on a sticky note or with lipstick on your bathroom mirror, for all I care. Do it however you want to do it, just as long as you do it. You'll be grateful you did. And there ya go—your first entry!

At the end of the day, life *can* be a bed of roses if you think about what a rose really is: a blossom, thorns, and a bud. After I do my gratitude entry for the night, I like to think about *my* rose. What was the blossom, or the best part of my day; what was the thorn, or the worst part; and what was the bud, or the thing I'm most looking forward to seeing bloom in the future?

These don't have to be big things (some days, it's "blossom: nailed my morning workout; thorn: spilled my coffee in the elevator; bud: getting a good night's sleep"), but the metaphor provides a nice moment of reflection on the small wins and losses that are inherent each day. I like to do this after taking a trip or wrapping up a big project, too. What were the best parts, which

I can celebrate and try to replicate in the future? What were the worst parts, which I can learn from and try to avoid? And what are the things I'm most looking forward to, to keep me moving, well . . . forward? After all, building a life you love means not just being grateful for where you are, but identifying what needs to change, and looking ahead to where you're going.

BUILD A LIFE YOU LOVE

It's your life. Live it how you want. I'm not going to judge you for what that looks like because after all, I'm not the one who has to wake up to your life every morning.

But I will challenge you, before we move on to figuring out your life goals and how to accomplish them, to ask yourself if you're living the life you love and loving the life you live *now*. Because if you're not, as Benjamin Button said, "I hope you have the strength to start all over again."

You can begin living a life you love and are proud of—one with purpose and meaning—at any point, even if you're starting over for the tenth time, but only if that's your intention.

CAN I GET YOUR INTENTION, PLEASE?

"What are your intentions with my daughter?" You've heard the father ask this question of potential suitors in countless TV shows and movies. Basically, he wants to know if the guy's gonna treat his girl well and put a ring on it or what?! But I have yet to see a show or movie where the heroine asks herself, "What are my intentions for me?"

In our story, we've already put a ring on it. So now it's time to live with the intention of treating ourselves well. The strength of the commitment you make to yourself determines how your life will turn out. Remember, this is not a shotgun wedding. We are in it for the long run.

Repeat after me:

I, (state your name), promise to define my values and live my life in accordance with them.
I promise to speak my truth, find my purpose, and not compare myself to others.
I promise to make choices that move me closer to my goals.
I promise to stay focused but be open to learning and changing.

If you value commitment enough to expect it from others, then you should be taking your commitment to yourself seriously. Are you committed to your values? If so, do you *act* committed to them? If not, how can you expect anyone else to be?

Setting intentions for yourself is an important step, but it's not the last one. It's like setting the table for your life. And, while I like a Pinterest-worthy place setting as much as the next girl, *living* with intention means actually eating at that table.

You may say you want to live a life of health and wellness, but if you're also getting lit every weekend, you're only cheating yourself. Of course, you can value whatever you want. If you value partying and boozing, then own that. But if you truly value health and wellness, then your life should have more juice than gin in it.

Not every day has to be a juice day. And there's definitely a time and a place to sip on gin *and* juice. But decide what kind of life will make you proud, and let that determine what you order to drink, because that drink will affect your future. The way you choose to fill every day and exert your energy will determine your life's direction. Where you end up next year or in ten years is determined by the choices you make now.

FIND YOUR WHY

It's okay if you've never thought to define your calling or question your contribution to the greater good. Today is as good a day as any to start asking yourself: "Why?" As in, beyond the day-to-day desire for success: "Why do you do what you do?"

THREE QUESTIONS TO ASK YOURSELF TO FIND YOUR PURPOSE

1. *Will you have a legacy?* You don't need to come up with a groundbreaking scientific discovery or win a Grammy to have a legacy. Maybe you established an innovative new process at your company or a thriving community garden in your neighborhood. What do you want to be known as—whether it's to the world, or to your future two-year-old?

2. *What will your eulogy say?* This might seem a little dark, but connecting with yourself existentially will help you to prioritize and gain perspective. Do you hear "She was a member of Congress who fought for women's rights"? Well, are you in Congress or planning to run at some point? Which rights are you fighting for?

3. *What makes you cry?* Think, "My purpose is
   . . ." and then start writing anything that comes
   to mind. Keep going. When you find yourself
   tearing up—ding ding ding! You've found it.
   Then, get after it. After all, a purpose without a
   plan is just a prayer.

As is my style . . . here's how I would answer these.
Especially with some of the more taboo subjects, sometimes it's just easier to see an example or for someone to
go first, so let that be me:

1. My legacy will be empowering a generation
   of young people—and especially women—to
   take control of their lives, careers, and finances
   once and for all, through books, TV shows,
   and online education tools that will thrive
   long after I'm gone.
2. When I'm gone, I hope to be remembered as
   a successful, self-made businessperson and
   journalist who was a champion for women
   and their careers, and a loyal friend who made
   the lives of those in my inner circle better for
   my friendship.
3. My purpose is to reach other women who have
   gone through hell and survived the fire, albeit
   with broken homes, abusive relationships, or
   mental disorders, and to empower them to find
   success—as they define it for themselves—not

by ignoring those challenges, but by learning from them, and owning them.

Of course, you can and should check in with these three questions on occasion, especially as your personal and professional goals change. And as your relationship with yourself deepens, you'll likely want to refine your answers as well. But let's start with today: What is your "why?" now?

We get asked what we do or ask someone else the same question at least, what, once a day? Instead of thinking of your "what," start to think about your "why." Yes, part of your "why" is to make money. You need money to live. But don't over- (or under-) state money's role in what you do. You don't get out of bed every single morning to greet the day "only for the money" or "not at all for the money."

FYI

A now-famous study from Princeton University found that $75,000 is the optimal annual salary for happiness. After that, studies have shown, your happiness doesn't increase much, even as your money mounts up to the billions. Can it make you happy? Well, it depends on how you spend it. Can money buy you meaning? No—and money without meaning is just paper.

Finding your "why" will also help to carry you through times when the "how" feels like a puzzle. It has with me. Do you ever get so frustrated that you hear yourself say, "How am I going to do that?!" or "What am I going to do?" out loud? I do. But I find that when I shift from "how" and "what" to "why," the questions become easier to answer and the answers become tougher to question.

WHAT DO YOU MEAN?

I'm not here to tell you the meaning of life (or get the Justin Bieber song stuck in your head). I'm here to give you a little kick in the booty on the way to finding it for yourself. Those who self-identify as having meaning and purpose in their lives are almost two times more satisfied at work and about one and a half times more engaged in their work than those who don't.

A fascinating study of hospital janitors by a professor at Yale University found that those who viewed their job as one that contributes to the goal of healing and helping people were happier overall, while those who saw their job as strictly those tasks outlined in their job description did not enjoy it. The happier group described themselves as part of a bigger team in the hospital and as working toward a greater good. The meaning of their work came from more than the thankless daily grind of "what" they were doing, which often involved, you know, cleaning up bodily fluids. It came from focusing on the "why" they were doing it: the impact it was having toward other people's health and wellness.

Some of the most successful companies choose to consciously focus on the meaning of what they do, too, rather than just on capturing the largest market share in their industry. You need look no further than their mission statements.

- **Facebook:** "To give people the power to share and make the world more open and connected."
- **Microsoft:** "To enable people and businesses throughout the world to realize their full potential."
- **Google:** "To organize the world's information and make it universally accessible and useful."
- **Nike:** "To bring inspiration and innovation to every athlete in the world. If you have a body, you are an athlete."

Now, Nike is the biggest, most lucrative athletic company in the world. But its mission statement is about chasing meaning, not just paper. It focuses on the influence Nike aims to have on the people it reaches. If Nike is successful in achieving that, then success will come. And, it has. With that formula, you can "Just do it," too.

MAYBE IT'S NOT THE JOB . . .

. . . maybe it's you. That probably sucks to hear, but it's a powerful thing to come to terms with, because it's also the only thing you can really control. So put down the magnifying glass and pick up the mirror. Sometimes, redefining "having it all" means finding a way to turn what you already have now into what you've always wanted.

There's a popular concept in positive psychology called "job crafting." It is essentially an exercise in taking the role you have now and making it your own instead of setting out to find another. Reframing what you're doing now makes it easier to change your mindset about it. "Crafting" your job can also get you thinking about how you fit into a larger framework, how you further a mission or have a positive impact.

When I first started working as a business news anchor, I hated business and finance. Seriously. I didn't understand it, and I felt uncomfortable talking about it. I thought it was just helping rich people get richer, which felt gross to me morally. All I thought about was how I could use my experience as a business reporter to get to my next job as an investigative reporter as quickly as possible, so that *then* I could really start making a difference.

The thing is: I *was* making a difference. I just needed to reframe the "why" of what I was doing. By reporting on how the world's markets were moving and reacting in real time, I had the opportunity to write the first draft of history. The economy, arguably, is the factor that makes the *most* difference in people's day-to-day lives. It determines whether or not we have jobs and what those jobs are worth. It impacts what we buy. When I stopped to think about it, *every* story went back to money. And I had insider access.

After I had that epiphany, I landed my dream job. Of course, it was the exact same job. It just *became* my dream job.

Here's how I went about transforming the job I had into the one of my dreams.

First, I listed what I imagined I would do in my "dream job":

- Report special series with my own franchise
- Uncover and investigate issues that mattered to people
- Educate and inform others through my storytelling

Then, I listed what I hated about my current job:

- Speaking to some scummy Wall Street people
- Too confined inside a studio
- The jargon and numbers

Finally, I listed what I loved about my current job:

- A boss who is my champion
- The ability to craft content
- Hours that are consistent (the market closes at 5 PM, and that's a wrap, folks!)

I sat with these lists. Having a boss who believed in me, the ability to craft content, and reliable hours were *exactly what I needed* to do the things on my dream job list. So I came up with a series idea: investigating business crimes. It fit my goal of uncovering issues that mattered, but also fell into the scope of my business beat. My boss liked it and gave me the freedom to work on it after the market closed. The series got me out into the field, allowed me to focus on people and not numbers, and would ultimately get picked up by more mainstream news outlets.

Boom. I knocked out the things I hated (and to be fair, there are scummy people and good people in every industry and walk of life). I played to the things I *did* love about my current job (you can always find something). And, within that framework, I made my dreams a reality.

It's so annoying to me when "experts" say things like "go follow your passion." Well, yes, that is sometimes possible. But I didn't have that luxury. I just needed a job, and I took anything

I could get to get ahead. If you can't "do what you love," then love what you do. By finding a way to passionately love the job I had, I did indeed end up "following my passion," just not the way—or the one—that I expected. Fast-forward more than a decade, and I've crafted a career I love by continuing to find ways to love the shit out of each and every one of the jobs and opportunities I've taken.

Your Title

In the same study about hospital janitors, two of the respondents considered themselves "a healer" and "an ambassador," respectively. Now, those job titles didn't go on LinkedIn, but you'd better believe that going into work to mop vomit off the floor becomes much more rewarding when you reframe your role as something awesome.

No one is going to do that for you—and no one even needs to know about it. Are you a "countess of communication," helping people stay in touch with their loved ones (working at the post office)? Are you a "sculptor of sales," shaping people's hearts and minds (working at an ad agency)? A "majesty of meetings," bringing people together to celebrate (as an event planner)?

BTW, if you want a royal title, for real, you can buy a ton of different ones online. (Yes, of *course* I've looked into this.) You can pay for a legit royal title, paperwork and all. But, being a "baroness" of whatever you do, in your own mind—and truly owning and loving that title—is way more valuable in the long run than any fancy title you can buy.

Think of yourself as one of the major companies I listed mission statements for, only in this case you're the CEO *and* the board of directors *and* the employee of the month. You're the head honcho of You, Inc. So, think about what *your* personal mission statement would be. I know you want to be successful (after all, you picked up this book!), but if you can verbalize *why*, you'll have more luck achieving that success, and it will feel more meaningful when you do.

Just like those companies' mission statements don't focus on "making bank," Emotional Wellness doesn't come from a big bank account (otherwise, everyone with money would be happy and emotionally well—and we know from the tragic death of Kate Spade and others like her that they aren't). It doesn't come from the city you live in, the car you drive, or the partner you have.

No matter where you go, how you get there, or who you are going with, there *you* always are. So, anytime you're tempted to say the words "you complete me" . . . do it in the mirror.

BOTTOM LINE

Conventional Wisdom: Taking care of yourself is selfish.

Being "selfless" is not a good thing. Taking care of your*self*, on the other hand, is a *great* thing. So, go ahead, be "selfish" and when someone calls you that, say "thank you."

Conventional Wisdom: The only way to live a life you love is to do what you love.

That sounds lovely, but it's not always possible. What *is* always possible is reframing the way you think about what you do, and loving that.

Conventional Wisdom: I just need to find the right person and then I'll be complete.

No. You complete you. Good talk.

HAVE YOUR CAKE AND EAT IT, TOO

Define What "Having It All" Is, Then Devour It

L et's say you get a piece of cake. Cool, now you have a piece of cake. Then, you eat it. Awesome. Nothing that special about having cake and then eating said cake, amiright?

When people say, "You can't have your cake and eat it, too," I want to smoosh a hunk of frosting in their face to shut them up. Um, hello, you *can* have your cake and eat it, too. You can actually do whatever you want with your cake—it's yours. You just can't do everything you might want at the same time.

The idea behind this clichéd cake analogy you've heard a thousand times is, essentially, that you *can't* have it all. In this step, I'll show you that you *can*. I will also tell you why you shouldn't follow conventional wisdom about the things you can or can't have in your life, but rather wise up about your own definition of "having it all."

WTF IS "HAVING IT ALL?"

The concept of "having it all" both inspires and angers me. The phrase can be traced to the title of OG Super Woman Helen Gurley Brown's book *Having It All: Love, Success, Sex, Money . . . Even If You're Starting with Nothing*. The book came out in 1982, when Ms. Brown had been at the helm of *Cosmopolitan* magazine for twenty years, and it was intended to be a tongue-in-cheek guide for women who wanted more of the best things in life for themselves. When I read it, her inspiring story of escaping a shitty upbringing to rise to the top hit close to home.

What angers me, however, is that the idea of "having it all," born from this kick-ass book that encouraged women to be sexually liberated, has been appropriated by TV, movies, and commercials into some unrealistic, punishing set of expectations for women. In the last three decades, this idea went from a much simpler concept of being able to have both a love life and a career to the notion that women have to be all things perfectly—a mom (which HGB wasn't, and didn't address in her book, BTW), a wife, a sex kitten, and a career rock star in equally measured parts.

Leading women's studies scholars point to the '80s "Because I'm a Woman" commercial for Enjoli perfume as the first depiction of the ideal we currently associate with "having it all." The campaign shows a woman singing: "I can bring home the bacon, fry it up in a pan, and never let you forget you're a man." It goes on to show the woman flip from "business" to "mom" to "sexy" attire: "I can work 'til five o'clock, come home and read your tickity tock, and if it's loving you want, I can give you the shivers."

Super Women . . . that was a cringe-worthy commercial. Career-oriented men who are also dads don't expect to attend every school function, make cupcakes for the bake sale, and look like a Calvin Klein underwear model while they do it. The difference is that we beat ourselves up a lot more for not "doing it all" than they do. "Having it all" is not about being equal parts PTA mom, master chef, seductress wife, and C-suite exec. "*Having* it all" doesn't mean "*Doing* it all." That's an impossible, unrealistic, Superwoman-like expectation that's a recipe for burnout.

We have to let go of the pursuit of trying to be Instagram-perfect in every aspect of our lives. It is draining our Emotional Wellness. Remember the stats from my survey: almost all of us (89 percent) feel we are on the verge of burnout, with more than two-thirds (71 percent) about to experience a breakdown. This endless pursuit of perfection in every single category does nothing for that ultimate pursuit—of happiness— and desire for balance.

Perfection doesn't work long term. Progress does. So, let's aim for that.

YOU CAN'T DO IT ALL

It's only natural to wonder where other women are in their lives, and to compare ourselves to them. We want to know: Do they "have it all?" The answer: Yes, some of them do. Just not in the way social media would lead us to believe it exists. And then we want to know this: How do they "*do* it all?" And the answer is: They don't.

No one has exactly your responsibilities and circumstances, and no one else combines those with precisely the same goals. If you are a working mom, looking to get promoted on the regular, comparing yourself to a stay-at-home mom who homeschools her kids and makes her own bread is not realistic. Neither is comparing your career to that of a single business phenom with a multibillion-dollar company, or your health regime to that of a fitness blogger. You can have all of those important pieces—being a good mom, career success, fitness—but you can't do it like women who have reached the highest levels in each of those areas, often by focusing on just that one thing.

I used to define "having it all" as being the best at everything. Well, that backfired. So I redefined and reclaimed it for myself. If your definition isn't working for you, it's time for you to redefine and reclaim your own version, too. Later in this step, we're going to hone in on our goals and start building our own definition of "all." You can also use *The Super Woman Journal* to keep you on track throughout the day so that you can see what you're focusing on now and forgive yourself for not doing the things you're not.

Take it from another OG Super Woman, former secretary of state Madeleine Albright. She said, "Our life comes in segments, and we have to understand that we can have it all if we're not trying to do it all at once." It was only after she got divorced that she started focusing on her career in a big way. While her academic life was taking off (she earned a master's and a PhD shortly after her third child was born), she was once asked to participate more at her kids' school, to which she said: "What in God's name does a woman have to be so that she doesn't have to worry about the carpool?"

You can do anything you want. You can run a mean carpool. You can run diplomacy for the free world. You can run a marathon a month. You just can't do it all at once.

PLEASE LEAN THE FUCK OUT

Sheryl Sandberg wrote the wildly popular book *Lean In*. She preached that women should "lean in" more, meaning dig in to work more and push harder. In theory, that can, well, work. In practice, I've found that it's not always the healthiest move.

CONFESSIONS
OF A SUPER WOMAN

The Time I Leaned In Really Hard

I'll never forget when I finally got the call from a Big Shot TV executive, someone I'd been asking (er, politely stalking?) for a meeting for months to talk about a new show pilot I was jazzed about. I had spent weeks building out a presentation pitching my idea, researching the subject, and carefully outlining the legal parameters for our partnership. I had really leaned into this project, putting it ahead of everything else—including my sleep, health, and personal life.

And then, there he was (well, there his assistant was) lighting up my iPhone screen. It wasn't just the cold February air that made my breath catch in my throat.

"Hi, Nicole. This is Zoe, from Mr. Big Shot's office. He took a peek at your pitch and would like to talk to you about the project."

"Wow, of course! I'm so flattered!" I said, looking around for a quiet spot to duck in, out of the cold and noise. "Is he available for a call tomorrow morning between, um, ten AM and twelve PM, or three to five PM?"

I was proud of myself for suggesting an actual date and time for the call, despite my excitement and frozen fingers. I knew that would show how assertive I was (and also, let's keep it real: I wanted the extra time to prep!).

"Actually, no, he's available right now. Okay for me to put him through?"

Shit. "Yes, of course!"

I picked up the pace (no small task in stilettos!), hoping I could make it back to my apartment before the small talk ended so that I could pull up the presentation on my laptop and go from my notes. But then:

"Hi, Nicole. It's Mr. Big Shot. I've taken a look at your pitch and have a few questions about the format. How many panelists would you suggest per show, and which of the guests you mentioned in your pitch can you get ahold of by Friday?"

My mind went blank. I tried to remember the details of the presentation, but no dice. Then, stalling, I talked through the show concept again—which was silly, since he had clearly read it already—all while breathlessly trying to pull up the deck on my phone with my numb fingers. Scrolling, scrolling . . . my adrenaline was high; my heart was racing. This was my opportunity, and I wasn't going to blow it. Ah, here's the PDF, finally! Loading, loading . . . almost there . . .

SMACK!

My feet flew out from under me, and I went down. Hard.

Turns out, black ice is super tricky to see, especially when you're staring down at your screen. Is it sad that the first thing I did when I came to was to reach around frantically for my phone? Well, it was—and it was pointless, as I found my phone a few feet away with the screen smashed into a million pieces.

If I hadn't been so fried and frazzled, I might have been able to remember the details of the presentation I'd worked so hard on, or at least stay calm enough to make a better impression. Instead I'd leaned way in, determined to make this opportunity a reality at all costs. I stressed out and sacrificed the other important parts of my life trying to make it happen. Did it blow up? Yes. Did I end up in the ER with a broken elbow? Yes. Did I hear from Mr. Big Shot again? Hell no.

While my injured elbow was painful, I knew it would be just fine. But healing from my harmful addiction to leaning in to every work opportunity like it was my last would be much harder. Having my arm in a sling for the next month wasn't fun, but it forced me to lean back (for a while, at least) in a way I likely wouldn't have otherwise.

"Lean back" or "lean out" doesn't mean "be lazy" or "compromise your goals." It means "make mindful choices about how you spend your time." Overextending and trying to do everything often results in actually accomplishing very little except for draining your energy and motivation. Take it from these Super Women who leaned all the way into burnout or near burnout territory:

- **Tiffany Haddish,** the comedienne, openly talked about her burnout only after she was criticized for bombing a New Year's Eve performance. She said, that year, she only slept in her bed twenty-eight days and worked almost every single day.

- **Lilly "Superwoman" Singh,** one of the most popular YouTube stars, announced to her fourteen million subscribers in 2018 that she needed a hiatus because of burnout. She said, "I'm mentally, emotionally, physically, and spiritually exhausted."

- **Selena Gomez,** the singer, actress, and most followed woman on Instagram, has been refreshingly open about her burnout. She took time off work and social media to focus on her health, saying that dialectical behavior therapy (or "DBT," which I will talk about in Step 12) changed her life.

- **Alexandra Ocasio-Cortez,** the youngest woman ever to be elected to Congress, has been outspoken about slipping into "eating fast food for dinner and falling asleep in my jeans and makeup" since entering politics. She said on social media that "we live in a culture where that kind of lifestyle is celebrated as 'working hard,' but I'll be the first one to tell you it's NOT cute and makes your life harder on the other end."

- **Hilary Duff,** the child star, has spoken honestly

about her bouts with burnout over the years. In 2005 she said, "It's the type of exhaustion that one night of sleep doesn't fix."

- **Beyoncé,** "the queen," has even struggled with burnout at different points in her career, canceling shows and taking a year off in 2011 to focus on her mental well-being.

We have to help each other heal from and break the cycle of burnout by pulling back the rhetoric of leaning in. While promoting her book *Becoming*, former first lady Michelle Obama said, "I tell women that whole 'you can have it all' [idea] . . . hmmm, nope, not at the same time, that's a lie. It's not always enough to 'lean in' because that shit doesn't work."

What she—the ultimate Super Woman—said.

GET IT ALL

In order to "have it all": 1) acknowledge that "having it all" and "doing it all" are not the same thing, and 2) define for *yourself* what "it all" means to *you*—then come up with an action plan to have *that*. You get to decide what that looks like for you and no one else. To achieve success, you have to set yourself up for it. If you don't define what winning means, you are destined to feel like you're losing even though you're not.

ANOTHER F WORD

As you know, I love me some F words. And as you may remember from my first book, *Rich Bitch*, I preached my three Fs of goal setting and planning: Finance, Family, and Fun. I encouraged you to come up with one, three, five, seven, and ten-year goals in those three areas of your life. I'm a big believer in first figuring out where you want to go in your life, and then reverse engineering to figure out how you are going to get there. I mean, you can't just jump in the car without knowing the address and expect to magically arrive at your destination.

A major ten-year study on goal setting found that only 3 percent of people set clear intentions and actually wrote their goals down. But, on average, those people earned ten times (!!) as much money as the other 97 percent.

FYI

When I first created those three Fs, I messed up. Mea culpa. It's not the first time, and it won't be the last. I forgot the most important F word: Fitness. And by Fitness, I don't mean a sick six-pack, I mean taking care of yourself—all of yourself: your physical wellness and your Emotional Wellness. Because, in fact, when your Emotional Wellness suffers, so does your physical, and vice versa. For instance, depression can lower your immune system, which means you get sick more often.

In failing to include Fitness in my grand plan of planning, I failed myself. And I'm not going to let that happen to you (or me) again. So, let's revisit my goals for the four Fs.

A lot has changed in the decade since I first started writing these down. (And, as I first discussed in *Rich Bitch*, we all maintain the right to adjust our goals as frequently as we want to, as long as we're creating a corresponding plan to get where we want to go.) I still suggest breaking each list down into one, three, five, seven, and ten-year goals. I like the shorter time frames because "What do you want to be doing in ten years?" can be a very daunting question. Those smaller, more manageable pieces make planning the future feel far less overwhelming and much more doable.

Finance

You probably have career goals in your head, but have you actually spelled out what they are? In order to hold yourself accountable, clear metrics are important. In my typical spirit, here are my current Finance goals first:

Year 1: Create a meaningful conversation and business verticals around *Becoming Super Woman*

Year 3: Launch a platform of e-courses

Year 5: Option my books into other mediums

Year 7: Pilot my own show about money and career issues

Year 10: Develop and host my own events series

And, look at that, I've already nailed my Year 1 goal (hey, reader!) and am well underway with my goal for Year 3. Having a clear outline for where I want my career to go has helped me to remain laser focused on getting there, even though I know I will adapt these goals as the industry I'm in changes and, of course, as I change.

Notice that Finance goals are not dollar amounts. Realistically, the money from your career should power the rest of your goals (unless you have a trust fund I don't know about). So as you flesh out the rest of the Fs, check back and see if your career choices cover what you want to achieve in all areas of your life. I recommend doing it this way because while it is cool to have actual money numbers as goals, whether it's a target salary or the bonus you're working toward, it's more constructive to determine what you would do with that money first. Based on that, you can determine what you really need instead of focusing on an arbitrary number like "a million dollars." If you need a million bucks for what you want to do, great. But, maybe you need more or less than that. You won't know until you determine the life you want to live.

As for spending that money, the sweet spot is somewhere between living like you're going to die tomorrow and believing you'll live forever. A similar principle applies to spending your time: you shouldn't put off your passions, but you still have to show up at the job that makes them possible. You want to enjoy the life you have now while making sure you also have the back of your future self. Our brains were developed to favor living in the present more than saving for the future because for most of evolutionary history we needed all of our resources to survive day-to-day. But while the jury is still out on the nuances of whether money can buy you happiness now or later, we know for sure that it *can* help you optimize for it. In order to do that, though, you need crisp clarity on what you want your life to look like in the near future and the long-term.

Family

Not a lot of business books talk about goal setting regarding family planning, but as one of my earlier mentors, MSNBC anchor Mika Brzezinski, drilled into my head, nothing is more money-, energy-, and time-consuming than having kids and/

or caring for family. And for women, not much else is more time-sensitive and affects your career more. In my case, I've adjusted my family goals more frequently than any of the other Fs, depending on who I met (or didn't meet). So, here are my Family goals today:

Year 1: Be in a committed relationship
Year 3: Have my first child
Year 5: Have my second child
Year 7: Consider having more children with the eggs I froze at age thirty-one
Year 10: Transition into an advisory role at work to travel and spend more time with my kids

It doesn't matter whether you want to have ten kids or ten cats, or whether you are caring for an elderly family member or are just trying to be more available to your friends, the point of this exercise is to outline what "having it all" looks like for *you*.

Fun

Lifestyle and fun goals are also an important part of what your complete "having it all" picture looks like. After all, living a full life means taking the time to hit the pause button and enjoying the fruits of your hard work. My Fun goals at age twenty-five were not so fun at all. I was a card-carrying workaholic, and only over time—and way too many beautiful summer weekends spent huddled over my computer screen in a dark apartment—have I learned to prioritize fun. For me, that comes mostly in the form of adventure travel. So, here are my Fun goals these days:

Year 1: Travel to a new country alone once a year—
in first-class

Year 3: Take a road trip once a month to a new town

Year 5: Start an annual girls' retreat somewhere fun
and active, like Bali

Year 7: Work and travel abroad for a few months a
year

Year 10: Buy a beach condo to spend summers in

Sure, fun is fun—but it can also be expensive and time-consuming (as any busy person who has tried—and failed—to book a proper vacation will tell you). Again, it's best to work backward. First, think about what kind of life you want. Do you want to take quarterly vacations? Monthly girls' weekends? Weekly date nights? Decide that first, then figure out what the dollar figure is to live that life.

Fitness

Of course, my F lists have changed a lot as life (and shit) happened. But what was missing—although it only became noticeable when I had my breakdown—was staying healthy in all aspects of the word. When I started this goal-setting exercise, I didn't even have Fitness as a category—and my physical and emotional health both suffered as a result. So, here's what my Fitness goals look like now:

Year 1: Go consistently to weekly psychiatrist
appointments

Year 3: Train for and run a half marathon

Year 5: Go on one retreat per year (i.e., a trip that's
totally centered around Emotional Wellness)

Year 7: Train for and run a marathon
Year 10: Attend a seminar or institute that teaches a
new skill or practice in mental health

Now, it's your turn to list out your four Fs: your goals for Finance, Family, Fun, and Fitness. Once you've come up with your answers, you've basically created a list of what "having it all" looks like for you. And if (when) you start to feel envious of others, go back and look at your list. Is it on yours now? Nope? Then, that's not what "having it all" looks like for you at this point in your story.

F YOURSELF

In order to set yourself up to reach your goals and get it all, you have to get it together and create a flight plan. One of the (many) nice benefits of having once dated a pilot is actually knowing what that looks like:

1. Find your destination. Check! We did that with our four Fs.
2. Figure out what you're working with, like storms and air traffic. (We will dig into how to identify and manage external challenges in Step 5.)
3. Create the best path to get to your destination based on the conditions, knowing that even the best plans have to change on, well, the fly. (And I'll talk about keeping a level head no matter what in Step 9.)
4. Get there. Fly your course while monitoring your controls, keeping 'er steady, and making sure you are

level with the ground along the way. (We will discuss
how to check in on yourself in Step 11.)

You don't have to know anything about planes to understand how to reach your life goals while dealing with real-life
complications. There is a lot of improvising as you go. But
improvising doesn't have to mean flying by the seat of your
pants.

Doing improv looks easy but (and I never thought I would
know this from firsthand experience) it actually takes a lot of
skill to make it look effortless. I've tried a ton of alternative
therapies and taken a ton of classes over the course of my journey to become a Super Woman and strengthen my Emotional
Wellness. One of the hardest was actually an Improv 101 class.
The class focused a lot on the basic rules of building a scene.
Yeah, I didn't realize improv had "rules," either, and I also didn't
realize how complex making people laugh could be. The gist of
the *Comedy Improvisational Manual*, created by Amy Poehler
and her team, I read (seriously) is that in every good sketch, you
must identify three things: 1) Who you are, 2) Where you are,
and 3) What you're doing. After you've determined *who* you are,
where you are, and *what* you're doing in an improv scene, you
need to convey those answers to the audience—ideally within
the first four lines of your skit. No pressure.

Since life is one big improvisation and a comedy (of errors)
of sorts, I started asking myself these questions as regular
check-ins off the stage, as well. Sometimes, when you ask yourself who you are, you'll find that what you want has changed,
and you need to chart a path to a whole new destination. More
often, you just need a course correction. Having clear goals is
great, but determining them is just the beginning. It's easy to get

blown off course—checking in with them and yourself ensures you're still heading in the right direction.

It's one thing for an actor (or *moi*, who was the one weirdo non-actor in the class) to know her part in the scene unfolding onstage; it's another thing to be able to articulate it clearly and quickly. But as soon as you do, the scene can go anywhere and everywhere you want to take it. There are no bad ideas. The only way it ends badly is if someone holds back. Doesn't go full out. Half-asses it.

The best shows (and lives) have full asses in them. And how do you get a full ass? Having cake. And eating it, too.

BOTTOM LINE

Conventional Wisdom: I can "have it all" if I work hard enough and never complain. Put up, or shut up.

You don't need to work like crazy at home and at your job, never breaking a sweat, in order to "have it all." I get asked the "How can I have it all?" question at pretty much every event I go to. "Easy," I say. "You decide what 'having it all' really means to *you* and then get that."

Conventional Wisdom: I've gotta do like Sheryl Sandberg and "lean in."

Don't go overboard "leaning in" or you'll fall over. *Lean In* also said that you need a good, supportive hubs or partner to "have it all." Well, that's not the most helpful advice for single moms who don't have one of those and can't afford a full-time nanny (or all the other luxuries wealth can buy you). What I've found more actionable is to "lean out" of the things I'm not focusing on right now and not shame myself for it. Perhaps we can start replacing the phrase "chillin' like a villain" with "chillin' like a superhero." I know it doesn't have the same lovely rhyme to it, but it's time to celebrate the dare I say heroic moments when you "lean back."

Conventional Wisdom: My goal is simple: be successful in all parts of my life.

Well, first of all, that's not simple. And, second, that's not a specific enough goal. If you don't know exactly where you're going, you won't be able to get there. You'll also set yourself up for failure by comparing yourself to others who are focused and specific about what they want.

STEP

4

IN BALANCE

*Create a Points System to Measure the Weight
of Your World*

The difference between "imbalance" and "in balance" is just a letter and a space. They even sound the same when you say them aloud—but they couldn't be more different. So which describes your life now? And which do you *want* to describe it? (*Hint: it's the latter.*)

Most people don't take the time to think about balance until they wobble. It's like walking across an actual balance beam. When you're confident and cruising along, you probably don't think about changing anything with your form. Sure, you might still wobble a little, but you keep your chin up, put one foot in front of the other, and keep moving forward. The easiest way to fall off the beam is to move your eyes from your point of focus, because as soon as you do, you lose your center of balance. Well, Super Woman, we aren't going to let that happen.

Even the most decorated gymnasts feel shaky sometimes. And because we know it's inevitable, the best way to minimize the wobble is to train. And we are (obviously) going for the gold at the Olympics of Balance. In the last step, you started looking ahead to figure out where you want to go. This step helps you stay balanced on your way there.

PEACE OUT, LADY JUSTICE

Some days, you stick to salad and take a hot yoga class, while other days, you opt for cupcakes and refuse to change out of sweatpants. That's balance, right? Well, sure, we've all been there and twice on Sunday. That kind of balance is delicious, but temporary. Finding the kind of balance that is consistent and sustainable takes a little more work.

The image we usually think of when we hear "balance" is a scale with two bowls, like the kind Lady Justice holds. Maybe this is why we tend to think in terms of balancing just two things. How many times have you heard the phrase "work/life balance"? I hate that term. First of all, since when is your life siloed? If you're not happy in one aspect of your life, you're not happy. Period. It's your *one* life. Second, I don't know about you, but my "work" is a pretty big part of my life. Thinking of your career as something standing in opposition to everything else in your world is guaranteed to make you miserable. Lastly, "life" is pretty damn vague. What about balancing a new relationship and your most important friendships, *plus* work and your burgeoning side hustle and your pottery passion? Is that "life/life/work/work/life balance"?! It's time to be done with the standard image we have of "balance." Go ahead, break that scale; the life of a Super Woman is too full to fit in only two categories anyway.

Balance looks different for everyone. That girl who practically lives at her office—definitely unbalanced, right? Not necessarily. Not only is balance not the same for everyone, balance isn't even the same for one person over time. For that girl right now, balance might mean putting 90 percent of her energy into her career. Ten years from now, that number might be 50 percent. It all depends upon what you value at any given time, what you want to achieve, and when you want to achieve it. You get to decide what "balance" means to *you* during each chapter of your life.

True balance doesn't mean spending exactly the same amount of time and energy on each area of your life all the time; but it also doesn't mean existing on coffee and no sleep all week and then crashing on the couch all weekend. When asked about how they stay balanced, a surprising number of the women I surveyed gave similar answers:

- "Treat myself to a deep-tissue massage once a month."
- "Stay in on a Saturday night and watch movies."
- "Sleep basically all day Sunday."

Listen, I love a good deep-tissue massage and a day to veg as much as you do. But real balance is not going all comatose and disconnecting on occasion. You can't try to quickly plug a leak in a sinking ship and expect to be seaworthy. Staying afloat demands your daily attention. Sure, we all have crazy days—or weeks—but aiming for regular balance will help keep the crazy times from driving you crazy over time.

MMMM, PIE . . .

I'm going to change the imagery you might associate with balance from a scale . . . to a tasty pie chart. I often muse about why in school we learned stuff like geometry and how to dissect a frog while skipping practical things like how to set and stick to a budget, but I will say that the lesson on the wonders of pie charts has come in handy.

We're going to balance a budget of sorts now—a budget of your time and energy. You can add or delete whichever categories you want a little later, but for now, let's start with five of the most common areas of our lives we value and try to juggle:

Career	
Romance	
Family & Friends	
Physical Health	
Emotional Wellness	
Total Points	

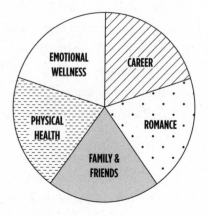

BTW, you'll notice that the categories fit nicely into our four Fs: Finance (career), Family (family & friends, romance), Fun (all of the above), and Fitness (Emotional Wellness and physical health). That's intentional; your goals should play into the choices you make about how to spend your day. Keep that in mind if you personalize the categories.

What I like about picking five to start out for this exercise is that there is less of an inclination to make them all even. Sure, you can evenly divide a pie into five pieces, like the one on the previous page, but it's not as easy as cutting the pie in half and giving one half to "work" and the other half to "life." Don't be a lazy bitch, use two categories, make them fifty-fifty, and call it a day. That's not realistic and will never account for the nuances of your life. There are nuances within "work" and "life," and those nuances will change. And that's good. That's the point. All areas of your life are not going to need equal attention at every moment. In fact, this pie chart will change all the time. Depending on major events in your life, it could change daily. Choosing your categories based on what you are focusing on and specifically value now will help you cut the pie more precisely and make better choices based on what you deem important. (If you want to keep track of what you're focusing on daily, you can do this with *The Super Woman Journal*.)

THE FIRST CUT IS THE DEEPEST

So, how we are cutting this pie today? Most exercises like this have you divide the pie by assigning each area of your life a percentage to reflect the weight it holds right now, with the percentages totaling 100 percent. I hate this conventional method. (Shocking, I know.) But I mean, come on: "Well, I would say 38 percent goes to career, 1 percent goes to romance (it's a dry spell), 8.5 percent goes to friends, 23 percent goes to physical health, and 29.5 percent goes to Emotional Wellness."

I rest my case. Instead, I'm going to give you some super fun points to play with! It's like the Weight Watchers system. You get ten points. You have your five categories. Now, divvy out those ten points into the five categories. Here's an example of how I would have first completed this exercise, years ago when my career was on the rise and my eventual breakdown nowhere in sight:

Career	7
Romance	1
Family & Friends	1
Physical Health	1
Emotional Wellness	0
Total Points	10

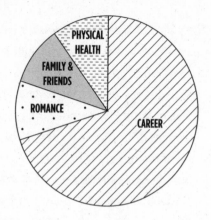

BTW, you can easily turn the points into percentages by simply adding a zero and a little "%" sign. Then if your brain likes the visual, draw based on those.

As you can see, I was working like all day, every day. I barely made time for dates or friends, and I worked out once in a blue moon. I certainly never did anything to help my mental health or develop a hobby. (I would have laughed at the suggestion of taking an improv class or going on a hike, two of my favorite things to do now.)

Now, your turn. Don't worry about the future, just focus on the now, and how many points each category is getting at this moment in time:

Career	
Romance	
Family & Friends	
Physical Health	
Emotional Wellness	
Total Points	10

I'll even give you a pie chart divided into ten pieces you can shade in to get a better visual of where things stand.

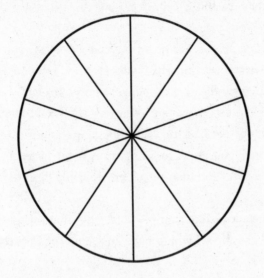

Now, what do you notice? There's no "right" answer here.

You could have given each of these categories exactly two points. Or you could have given all the points to romance if you're living in a real-life version of *The Notebook*. (Speaking of, Super Woman Elizabeth Gilbert, who wrote *Eat Pray Love* and has a thing for Bali like I do, said, "to lose balance sometimes for love is part of living a balanced life.") I don't care how you slice this pie, as long as the way you slice it is right for you (with one exception, which I note below).

To determine whether it *is* indeed right for you, answer these two questions:

1. *How do you feel when you review your points?* Do you feel empowered? Resentful? Do you feel overwhelmed just trying to allocate enough points to the

part of your life that you know, deep down, is under-served? Notice how you feel—free of judgment—and then use those feelings to make any necessary tweaks to your pie.

2. *How do you feel about the categories?* Do you have extra points for which you can't find a home, which might indicate a missing category? Do you want to add one? Or, is there a category you want to take out altogether because it just doesn't pertain to your life since you aren't focusing on it now? Listen to that reaction and then switch 'em up if you need to.

For the allocation example I just gave, that was pretty much all work, here's how I would have answered those questions:

1. I was okay with the point allocation. I didn't see a huge need to prioritize anything but my career. Of course, in hindsight, I really needed to give at least one point to Emotional Wellness. That's actually the only requirement I will give you for this exercise, because if you give nothing to that category for too long, it can and will demand all ten points eventually, like it did for me.

2. I was into these particular categories because I wanted to include all of these things in my life in a meaningful way, and I hoped that I would move toward them, even with very different points allo-cated to each. Now, if I decided I wanted to be a nun in the future, I would change things up and elimi-nate the romance category altogether. No judgment if that's what you're into.

CONFESSIONS
OF A SUPER WOMAN

Finding True Fitness

My Super Woman she-ro, Lavinia Errico, is the founder of Equinox. She is the ultimate self-made Boss Bitch who built one of the most recognizable brands in the fitness world. Her dream was to sell her company for a lot of money, and she did. But soon after, Lavinia plunged into a two-year-long battle with depression.

"My whole identity was wrapped up into the company. Without it, I didn't know who *I* was," she told me. "I never felt so alone, scared, and unsure of myself. I had been working my ass off since I was fourteen and without the grind I was lost."

For years she had focused only on physical fitness, but after selling her company, she began a journey to finally incorporate the mental and emotional fitness she'd ignored for too long. During that time she tells me she found "her truth," or who she was without any of the external factors like "being the founder of Equinox." She resliced her pie and gave her own Emotional Wellness, which had been starved for years, the largest piece for the first time.

"Sitting with myself to find my truth wasn't easy but it wasn't the hardest part. The hardest part is living in accordance with it," she says. "People still ask me all the time, 'Where is the old Lavinia?' and I say, "Oh, you mean the one who would put you first before me? She's long gone."

It's cool to use the same five categories I did, and it's cool if you think all of the categories need to change to reflect your values. Change them. Change them back. Change them again. You can value anything you want: education, fame, impact, public service, religion, wealth, and on and on. Your categories don't reflect *my* truth. They reflect *your truth*.

Knowing your truth inside out is a big part of living in balance. But the most important part is staying true . . . to your truth. Each day life gives you choices for how to spend your time. And each day you and only you get to choose how you want to do that. There can be endless options or at least enough to make your head spin. To not feel wobbly when it does, go back to your values. If you actually value what you say you do, the choices become easy and falling becomes hard.

THE FUTURE IS FEMALE

The first time I actually completed my balance exercise, I knew I wanted to use those same categories, but I wanted them to carry different weights. In fact, I knew that they *had* to carry different weights, because my goose egg next to Emotional Wellness had come back to bite me. My priorities had changed since those days focused only on sprinting up the network news ladder. So, following my breakdown, I allocated what I wanted to work toward in the next couple of years, over-indexing on Emotional Wellness to make up for the deficit I had. Here's what my exercise looked like shortly after I left the hospital (in the hospital, of course, all ten points had needed to be in the Emotional Wellness category):

Career	1
Romance	1
Family & Friends	1
Physical Health	2
Emotional Wellness	5
Total Points	10

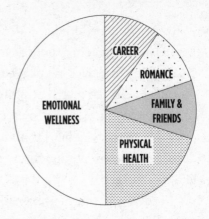

Throughout the book, I will unpack in great detail all the ways I discovered of adding more to the Emotional Wellness category of my life. That category is the crust in this analogy; you can fill your pie with anything you want, but without the crust, it will all fall apart. Do whatever you like with your pie, but remember that real Super Women always have at least one point in the Emotional Wellness column.

I hope you're still hungry, because now it's time to slice another pie. This is the pie of the future. Here's what I'm working toward these days, now that my breakdown is in the rearview mirror and I'm in a more balanced place:

Career	3
Romance	3
Family & Friends	1
Physical Health	1
Emotional Wellness	2
Total Points	10

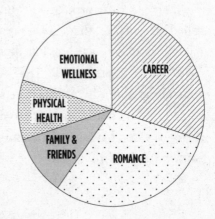

You might be thinking: "Maybe there's a typo here, because Lapin's list is changing about as much as a single drop of Botox changes my face. Not a lot." Well, it's not a full-on facelift, but it's a slight change that *I* certainly know is there. The tweak in this most recent pie chart puts just a little bit more emphasis on trying to see whether I want to have a baby. And, if I do (or don't), my current pie and future pies will change yet again, just like yours will.

Super Men (yes, they exist too!) don't think about balance or babies as much we do. They just don't. But we have to, if we want them. When we reach a stride in our career in our thirties, that's also typically when we crave that bun in the oven. Again, I don't care if you want to have ten of those buns or none. But I do care that you decide and plan how they will fit into your life if and when you have them.

That just means Super Women have more creative slicing to do than Super Men. It also means we have to commit to pulling our pies out of the oven more often to make sure they still taste the way we want them to. Nothing you can do with your pie is "bad" as long as it's to your liking. No one else is tasting it but you.

There's a hilarious Amy Schumer skit (redundant, I know) called "I'm so bad" that shows a group of women around a table talking about eating things like dessert and fries and saying how "bad" they are for doing it. The only thing that's bad is beating yourself up about living your life your way, because you think you should be doing something else or because everyone else is. So, let's stop having eater's remorse: eat that fucking pie, and enjoy it (along with all that cake we had in the last step).

BOTTOM LINE

Conventional Wisdom: I'll be balanced when [the kids move out, I get a new job, insert whatever excuse here].

People think balance is impossible, but I think it's their definition of balance that makes it so. There is no such thing as a "perfect" balance, and balance isn't something you achieve once and then have forever. There are always going to be new demands on you (and more excuses you can make to avoid balancing things). Instead of giving up on balance because it doesn't look like "what it's supposed to," keep rebalancing and shifting allocations as you go.

Conventional Wisdom: I feel unbalanced, but I do yoga!

Yoga is great exercise and can be a relaxing activity if you're into it, but you're not balanced *just* because you get down with downward dog. If you're feeling unbalanced, then, my yogi princess, you've got to strengthen your core, and I don't mean your abs—I mean those sweet Emotional Wellness skills.

Conventional Wisdom: Life balance means equally distributing your time between all parts of your life.

Balance is whatever you make it, as long as you're aware of what you're focusing on now and what your priorities are for the future. Stop being hard on yourself for not focusing on things you've actively decided you're not going to focus on at a certain time. Plus, the amount of time you might spend worrying about not being balanced, you could use to um, be more balanced.

5

BOUNDARIES, BITCH

Just Say Yes to Saying No

"My dance space, your dance space" is perhaps one of the best lines in perhaps one of the best movies of all time, *Dirty Dancing*. The main character, Baby, has "spaghetti arms" and keeps collapsing her frame while the Bad Boy Hottie, played by Patrick Swayze, is trying to teach her a formal dance. He shows Baby how to hold her stance (and her own) by explaining that the two of them each have their own area to dance in, and to make the dance work, dancers must respect each other's boundaries.

You might think, from a movie called *Dirty Dancing*, that the "dancing" would just be bumping and grinding all over each other. But what Baby learned in the film is that the dirtiest dancers are also the most rigorously trained. And the best rule breakers are the ones who know the rules before breaking them intentionally.

In case you can't tell, I love *Dirty Dancing*, and I also love . . . dancing! A little-known fact about me is that I'm classically trained in ballet. I actually went to a performing arts high school in Los Angeles to study dance before finding my calling in TV news. Dance taught me that you can't be a good partner if you can't hold your own. Partners can offer support, but they can't prop you up or do your part for you. In the previous step, you set up your "dance space" by determining what matters to you most. In this step, I'm going to help you protect your "dance space" from your "partner," whether that person is an actual romantic partner or a colleague, boss, friend, or family member. Dancing that looks effortless takes some effort up front. So, let's cha-cha, baby.

BORDER CONTROL

Boundaries are limits that define your personal space. We understand geographical boundaries as lines that mark the limits of countries or states. Personal boundaries do the same thing. We might say, "you crossed the line," meaning that someone has violated our boundaries, usually by saying or doing something grossly offensive. But the "line" or boundary you draw isn't just to protect you from egregious oversteps. Boundaries can and should also be distinctions between acceptable behavior (to you) and any behavior that compromises your Emotional Wellness.

You know *roughly* where the line is in various areas of your life, right? But would heads of countries be cool with it if their borders were *roughly* drawn? I. Don't. Think. So. You shouldn't be either.

So let's define and set some clear boundaries so you can fill in the rest of the map. How would you finish the following sentences?

Others cannot: _____
_____
_____
_____

I have the right to ask for: _____
_____
_____
_____

To value myself and my time, I can: _____
_____
_____
_____

I'll go first. My sentences look like this:

Others cannot: *make judgments about my family history, make fun of mental health issues, or wrongly accuse me of something.*
(Other examples: *scream at me, get physical toward me, tell racist jokes, put me down, try to embarrass me in front of others, make comments about my size, go through my email or texts without me knowing.*)

I have the right to ask for: *help when I need it, alone time, and affection.*
(Other examples: *another dish when mine is prepared incorrectly, silence in an Uber, quiet time during a facial or massage, help with housework, a customer service supervisor.*)

To value myself and my time I can: *keep "me time" sacred, stay in when I am too tired to go out, and say "no" when I don't have time to do something.*

(Other examples: *cancel plans when I'm sick, return text messages and emails on my own timeline, go on a trip without inviting or telling a friend, change my mind when something doesn't feel right.*)

Your personal boundaries are like your bill of rights. What do you have the right to do? What do you have the right to expect from others? It doesn't matter what your bill of rights includes, as long as you act in accordance with what it says.

Live Like You Were Dyin'

It might sound morbid, but any time you're tempted to give some of your precious time away to something you don't want to do or something you don't feel good about for whatever reason, pause to think about how much actual time you have on this earth. Consider a specific example of something you love to do and think about how many more times you have left to do it. Say you're forty, and you ski once a year. Well, the life expectancy for an American woman is currently seventy-eight . . . meaning you have just thirty-eight more chances to hit the slopes (or the ski lodge after a certain age). Start thinking of how few chances and little actual time you have to do the things you love and watch how it changes your perspective on things you don't.

DRAW THE LINE

If you're working for someone else, you probably think that your boundaries are not up to you. But whether you're a VP, entrepreneur, or just starting out in your career, you can and should set professional boundaries. Drawing the line at the office will not only help your own sanity, it will make it easier for you to keep your promises and earn you the respect of others.

Let's do the same exercise we just did, but this time specifically for work:

Professional relationships cannot: _____

_____

_____

_____

I have the right to express: _____

_____

_____

_____

To do my best work, I need and have the right to ask for:

_____

_____

_____

I'll go first again. My sentences look like this:

Professional relationships cannot: *be passive-aggressive.*
(Other examples: *make me feel bullied, intimidated, or silenced; become sexual; sabotage my work; overwhelm me with communication or gossip.*)

I have the right to express: *when I feel like I am unable to accomplish something asked of me.*
(Other examples: *when I am unable to answer something on the spot; my goals and ambitions.*)

To do my best work, I need and have the right to ask for: *space to stay laser focused on the task in front of me.*
(Other examples: *help from others, help with resources, advice, and mentorship.*)

Setting professional boundaries doesn't mean that you have to be super rigid or tough. Give yourself some wiggle room to get involved with new adventures, projects, and deeper professional connections (and understand that sometimes you have no choice but to say "yes" to that urgent task your boss just assigned you). Keep the context in mind. If a colleague has an issue and genuinely needs your help, the Super Woman thing to do is help a sister out. But, if this becomes a regular thing and starts to eat up your time or makes you uncomfortable, then you gotta tell that woman to fly on her own.

Remember, while no one wants to feel uncomfortable, "uncomfortable" means something different to everyone. Think about what makes *you* "uncomfortable." If your threshold for "uncomfortable" is high, then don't pretend like it's not.

If you're actually totally cool crafting your boss's kid's science fair project, and that doesn't make you uncomfortable whatsoever, that's fine. Or maybe it's not fine, and you know that in your gut you don't feel right doing it. Figure out your personal comfort zone first, so you can draw your own boundaries in a way that makes sense for you.

Just like little kids test boundaries to see what they can get away with, the people you work with and for will test yours. So will your friends, family, and even significant other. What can they get you to say "yes" to? How much of your time and energy can they push for?

The boundaries you set and enforce—or don't—set up a framework that guides people on how to treat you. If you keep saying "yes" indiscriminately, why *wouldn't* someone keep asking you to do something? I would.

CONFESSIONS
OF A SUPER WOMAN

It's Not About the Horse

"I'll go."

I raised my hand first in the "equine therapy" class I signed up for at Miraval, a wellness retreat in Arizona. I thought I was going to be spending time petting and riding all the pretty horses, which sounded therapeutic (otherwise why would it be on the menu of "wellness" activities?). But as I soon discovered, equine therapy, at least this particular version, had nothing to do with *riding* horses.

"This class is all about boundaries," the instructor said as she used a training whip to guide the horse around the ring. "So all I want you to do is walk the horse around a circle with intention. The horse will feel that energy but only from a comfortable distance of a few feet, not too close and not too far, and follow your lead if you're strong enough in your conviction." That's right. It seemed like a joke to me, too, but the whole class was about walking a horse . . . in a circle. That's it.

I got this, I thought as I entered the ring under the instructor's watchful gaze. I stroked the horse's face, saying "I got you; we got this" a few times. Of course, I knew the horse didn't understand all that, but I figured if I could quickly make him my best friend, he would let me easily guide him around in a circle.

"You can stop petting the horse," said the instructor, interrupting my whispering sweet nothings to the beautiful creature. "Do you often try really hard, sometimes too hard, to get people to like you?"

Oh shit, I thought. *This is about to get real.*

"The horse doesn't understand English. The only thing that makes the horse move with you is your energy and intention; it's communication boiled down to its most basic level. That's the only language he understands and the only way for you to tell him where to go," the instructor (slash therapist, as quickly became apparent) said as she handed me the whip.

I cracked it against the ground, still baby talking to the horse—even though intellectually I knew that it wouldn't help—and moving in closer. Then I stood in front of him, saying "come on" as I swayed in the counterclockwise direction the instructor had led him before. But the horse started meandering in the opposite direction.

"Can I take him clockwise instead?" I asked. "That's the direction he seems to want to go, and I want to do what he wants."

"Sure," she said. "But do it because you want to, not because you think he wants to."

I followed the horse as he turned slightly clockwise and then tried to get him to trot in that direction with me. No luck. In fact, he started meandering back the other way. This was wayyyyy harder than I'd thought.

"Gah, okay, I guess I'll take him counterclockwise again," I said, growing sweaty and nervous and feeling like I totally sucked at this.

"Do you often try to make people happy and put their needs before your own?" the instructor asked. All of a sudden there was a lump in my throat—the kind you get when you're about to cry but trying not to.

"C'mon, let's go here. This way!" I said to the horse. I was still trying to be gentle and soft so that the horse would like me, and I moved in even closer.

"You're moving in too close to the horse," said the instructor. "You need to keep a boundary and be decisive so that he can see and feel what you want him to do."

I scooted back and then stopped. The horse came to me.

"Oh, see, he likes me. He's not mad at me," I said, turning to face the instructor. As I did, the horse walked away.

"Do you have trouble setting and maintaining boundaries, Nicole?" the instructor asked. "You're coming in too close and not making enough noise with the training whip to get his attention. He doesn't understand what you want. If you don't know where you want to go, or keep changing your mind, the horse can't trot with you."

I couldn't stop the tears as I tried again and again to lead the horse. I didn't want to leave the ring until I got it right. The closest I came was getting the horse to trot halfway around the circle with me before cutting a corner. The same corner every time.

"I'm so bad at this," I wailed, unable to close the floodgates. "He keeps wanting to bail and leave me just when I thought we were doing so well."

"Do you fear abandonment and beat yourself up when it happens?"

WTF, was I all of a sudden on *Dr. Phil*??

I wanted to go hide back in my room. I was embarrassed for bawling and making a scene. But I also wanted to stay until I'd completed a full circle with the horse.

You're not a quitter, I told myself over and over again.

"Do you often think things are your fault when they don't work out?" the instructor asked, as I kept trying.

"Yes, I do, and when they leave I think it's all my fault," I said, catching myself saying "they" and realizing it was pretty clear that I wasn't talking about horses.

"See, it's not about the horse. The horse is a mirror of you. The horse will go wherever you want it to go as long as you know exactly where that is and can powerfully communicate that," the instructor said to me, better analyzing my relationship patterns in ten minutes than I had in a lifetime. "But it doesn't seem like you do."

I didn't. I sobbed and felt defeated. I never did complete that full circle.

"Should I try it one last time?" I looked back at the horse and the instructor once more as I neared the gate. My hands shook as I fumbled to open the latch, partly because I was worked up but mostly to buy time because I wasn't sure if I should really leave.

"There will always be more classes and more horses. Come back when you feel ready. You just have to be prepared to put your energy in the direction you decide, keep a certain boundary, and hold your ground so strongly that nothing the horse does can shake you. Remember, it's not about the horse, it's about *you*."

Everything important I know about boundaries, I learned from a horse. Now, you don't have to sign up for equine therapy to set boundaries. But you do need to understand them and know where yours are in order to lead life on your terms.

PUT UP A FENCE

There's an old adage: "Good fences make good neighbors." Well, I didn't realize the reason I had so many bad "neighbors" (relationships) was because I didn't have a good fence (or any fence at all). We will talk more about healthy relationships in Step 10, but before you invite any neighbors over, you need to get your own house in order.

Does this interaction sound familiar?

Friend: "Hey, I know we've been trying to get together for a while. My schedule has been slammed. Can you do breakfast tomorrow at 8 AM?"

You: "That works!" (Actually, 8 AM was the time you'd scheduled your workout.)

Okay, so unless this friend is the OG Super Woman Oprah herself, then your workout is your workout is your workout. It's on your calendar, and the guest of honor is you. Don't skip it. Even Oprah has said, "You have to be able to set boundaries, otherwise the rest of the world is telling you who you are and what you should be doing."

So, what about this instead?

Friend: "Hey, I know we've been trying to get together for a while. My schedule has been slammed. Can you do breakfast tomorrow at 8 AM?"

You: "No, I can't. I have a meeting scheduled then. Can you do noon?"

You're not lying here. In the first scenario, you canceled a meeting *with yourself* to avoid canceling on someone else. Why? Do you value that person's time more than you value your own? Do you value not letting them down more than you value yourself? I used to answer "yes" to those questions. Then, I started taking my own needs just as seriously as I would anyone else's.

In the second scenario, you value *you* first, and then find ways to work others into your schedule. Start thinking of saying "no" to someone else as saying "yes" to yourself. Turning down things that aren't priorities opens you up to the things that are.

THE SUPER ENFORCER

There's no need to clap back when someone encroaches on a boundary (don't forget, they're not psychic and may do so unintentionally). A calm, clear, and concise response is better than an emotionally driven diatribe. But boundaries are meaningless if you don't enforce them. Being wishy-washy is confusing and being confusing is weak. So, speak strongly to look strong.

For example: You keep getting asked to take on projects, your workload is overwhelming, and you are beyond stressed.

The wrong move is to say "yes" if you don't have the available bandwidth to do another task; an even worse move is to say "yes" passive aggressively, or "maybe" when you know it would take a miracle. There's an oft-repeated business saying that goes, "If it's not a 'hell yes,' then it's a 'no.'" That means, if it's a "maybe," then it's a "no." If you work for yourself, noticing when your immediate reaction is a "maybe" will be a litmus test for which people to work with and what projects to take on, especially if your inclination is to say "yes" to everything. If you work for someone else, checking your reaction can help you assess whether or not you can realistically take on more work.

The right move when you are asked to take on something new and are already overwhelmed is to tell the person simply and clearly that you can't commit to it at this time. This sounds obvious, but we are often so concerned about being nice and not hurting people's feelings that we tie ourselves into knots trying to find a way to say anything but "no" to avoid disappointing them. But most people at work, especially your superiors, will appreciate your honesty about your resources—it's way less "disappointing" than having you overcommit and do a shitty job.

Superwoman wants to help everyone all the time. Super Women know that time is their most valuable asset. And they invest it in themselves first.

It took me years—decades, really—to realize that investing in myself was critical for my overall success. Trying to do everything meant I didn't do anything well. And, trying to be everything to everyone meant I was nothing to myself.

Super Woman Shonda Rhimes said it best when she said, "No is a complete sentence."

SAYING "NO" WITH A SMILE

I get it. You have an insane job? Five kids? Fifteen parrots? Whatever it is, we all have stuff—stuff to get done, stuff to manage—and, ideally, we want to do all of said stuff successfully. Well, guess who decides if that happens? "Lapin, you're going to say it's up to *me*, again, but there are other people and responsibilities in play!! You're just not right this time."

Au contraire ma petite Super Femme! Lapin makes it happen. And you do, too. You are the one who says "yes" or "no" to anything and everything in your life (there are even ways to do that on the j-o-b, which I'll get to in a bit). Do you feel "obligated" to do something? If the answer is "yes," ask yourself: "*why*"?

You're a Super Woman and a lot of people will want your super self at their parties, on their committees, and heading up cool projects. Wanting to say "yes" to all of that is not wrong. But saying "yes" just to please people and make them like you is. Say "yes" all day long if you want—but only if it's right for you and pleases *you*.

Saying "yes" to things you are not stoked about out of a sense of obligation is *no bueno* in general. But, it's even worse when it eats into your "me time" and undermines your obligation to yourself. Making plans with yourself *is* making plans. You are your own party, your own committee, and the queen of your own projects. Say "yes" to *those* all day.

Saying "No" at Work

Being the DIY-do-it-all-chronic-overachievers that we are, we want to crush any commitment we make, especially at work. But if your current commitments (including the one you've made to yourself) will suffer from taking on *more* commitments, then instead of crushing anything, you're gonna *get* crushed. I get it: As you move up in your career, you don't always have a say in what comes your way. But you do have a say in how you manage your own bandwidth and other people's expectations (even your boss's!).

So, the next time you're faced with another commitment that you know you just can't take on, try this tactic:

Your boss: "Nicole, I'm looking for someone to update the handbook we give to incoming interns to reflect our latest projects and thought you might want to take this on. Can you do it?"

You: "Thanks so much for thinking of me—this sounds like a valuable project for our team! However, I am already committed to Projects A and B and want to keep my focus there so that I can knock those projects out of the park before our deadline. I do have a handy outline that I created regarding our new social media approach, which I will send to you by the end of the day to include in the handbook."

Your boss: "That's great; I had no idea you created that. However, I still need you to update the handbook. Can you have it back to me, incorporating your social media outline, by Friday?"

You: "I understand, and I want to make sure I have enough time to complete the handbook in a thorough manner on top of my other projects. Is a Monday deadline acceptable?"

Your boss: "Yes, that works."

You: "Thanks again for offering this project to me, and please do keep me in mind for future projects."

Why this works:

- Notice the "thank-you sandwich" we created here, starting with appreciation for the opportunity and finishing by expressing interest in being kept in the loop about future projects. Not only is this a gracious approach to negotiating with someone who holds a higher position than you do, but it also goes a long way to ensure you won't be passed over for a future opportunity that you might actually want.

- Present actual examples of what else you have cooking, like Projects A and B. This isn't meant to be defensive, but to demonstrate the many other ways you are contributing to the good of the team.

- When possible, refer the asker to a helpful resource or provide additional information to help move their project along—and solidify your status as a total team player. And offer an actual deadline for your contribution, which makes it more genuine. Of course, your boss has the right to refuse your amended deadline, but you won't get the extension unless you ask.

SUPER WOMAN TIP

Speak Up, Super Woman

I call bullshit on the phrase "women just need a seat at the table." I mean, sure, we need a seat. But, we also need a voice.

Studies have shown that in group projects, men do less but get more credit for the work they do. And, how do they do that? Well, it's partly due to them picking a task that is most likely to be highlighted. It's often assumed that when a person speaks for the team or answers questions, for example, that they have the most responsibility, ownership, or knowledge of the project. In reality, those who speak on behalf of a team aren't necessarily those who put in the most time or work, but their vocal roles lead to the perception that they have, and thus they receive greater recognition.

So, sign up for less but speak up more.

Saying "No" to Friends and Acquaintances

Being a good friend doesn't mean saying "yes" to everything someone asks of you. Now, if a friend is in need, that's one thing. But not every request can be an emergency. And you don't have to feel bad about being thoughtful about those that aren't. Consider this:

Your neighbor: Hey, Nicole! I'm putting together a weekly book club with some of the other women in our building and thought you might be interested in hosting at your place. Are you able to?

You: Wow, thanks so much for thinking of me—I'm

flattered! My schedule doesn't allow for hosting right now, but I'd love to join you when I can. Have you thought about introducing a theme to tie all of the books together? I'm very into mindfulness books at the moment!

Your neighbor: I hadn't thought of that, great idea!

You: Let me know if you find a host, and keep me posted on the schedule.

Your neighbor: Will do, thanks!

Why this works:

- Just because you have to pass on the "big" ask, doesn't mean you have to pass altogether (unless this is something you really *don't* want to do—but I'd say a women's book club about mindfulness sounds pretty fun, no?). Put the ask on your terms, but be genuine about it. So, if you turn down hosting in favor of occasional attendance, make sure you actually, um, show up every once in a while. Otherwise it's best to just politely decline fully to preserve the vitality of the relationship—and your own. Actress Gabrielle Union once said, "I swear to God, the second I learned to say 'no,' that was the best anti-aging I could do for myself."

- In this case, the fewer details about why you can't commit, the better. ("My schedule doesn't allow for hosting . . .") You live in close proximity to this person, so you don't want to provide specific examples, which they might in turn hold you to. ("Hey, Nicole, I thought you said you were working late?!")

- Again, offer up a useful resource or idea to help move the asker's project along.
- Note: Notice that I didn't suggest "asking Maria, who lives up the hall." You might know that Maria is a fabulous cook who loves to host, but you likely *don't* know what else she has going on. So don't put another Super Woman on the spot like that.

Saying "No" to Your Sig-O

Falling for someone is distracting enough. But is your partner trying to commandeer your calendar? You can turn him or her down without entering breakup mode. Here's how:

Your Sig-O: "My buddy is having some people down to his beach house this weekend. Wanna cut out early on Friday and party with us through Sunday?"

You: "That sounds like fun! However, I have that deadline on Friday, so I won't be able to leave early. I've been enjoying our time together on the weekends so much, but now I need some "me time" to take care of a few things."

Your Sig-O: "It's the weekend, babe, live a little!"

You: "I'm going to stay put, finish my work, run some errands, and spend Saturday rock climbing with the girls.

But I'm free on Sunday and would love to join you and your friends for a beach day. I'll meet you down there in the morning with my bocce set!"

Why this works:

- You've asserted that your work and your time are valuable, and that you're the kinda girl who crushes deadlines. If that's not sexy, then I don't know what is.
- You've also subtly reminded him of the quality time you've been spending together lately . . . so much that it's cut into your adulting and extracurriculars. Notice that you did *not* (and should not) apologize in this situation or give in to his pressure. Getting your shit done, at work and otherwise, is nothing to be sorry for. Save the "sorrys" for actual fights.
- By offering to join the group on Sunday morning, you demonstrate that you can be flexible, and you know how to have a good time. The day-trip gesture reaffirms your commitment to spending time with him. On your terms.

Saying "No" to Your Family

It's an unwritten law of nature: no one has more power to guilt you into doing something you don't want to do than your mother (or other close family member). There is a lot to be said for answering the call of family, but sometimes your duty to yourself is greater. Try this:

Your mother: "Aunt Susan tells me you haven't RSVPed to your second cousin Rachel's baby shower next Sunday. I assume you're still coming? I'll pick you up at 10 AM."

You: "I'm not able to make it next Sunday, and I actually just got off the phone with Aunt Susan to tell her."

Your mother: "What do you mean you're not coming?? This is Rachel's first baby! And you two were so close growing up . . ."

You: "I'm thrilled for Rachel, and I sent her a gift from her registry so that she has something from me at her shower. However, Rachel and I have hardly spoken since first grade. My weekend time is limited these days, so I have to prioritize how I spend it."

Your mother: "Well, alright . . . Can we still meet for coffee at 10 AM, before I go to the shower?"

You: "Of course! Looking forward to it."

Why this works:

- When it comes to family, sometimes you've gotta go the extra mile to avoid hurt feelings and drama. So, when letting a family member down, call (or at least attempt to). The personal touch of your voice (or voice mail) will go a long way to remind them that they're important to you. Don't give a million excuses as to why you can't be there; just decline the invitation graciously with "I'm not able to make it next Sunday" and leave it at that.

- If you're able, send a thoughtful gift or card in lieu of your attendance (whether it's a baby shower or wedding or birthday party). It doesn't have to be elaborate, but it will remind that person that you're thinking of them on their day (as well as reminding any judgey relatives who *are* there that you didn't just forget, thank you very much).

- Your mother might remember you and Rachel as little girls, but that was a long time ago. Define the relationship in present-day terms, and then assert your right to set your own priorities as the grown-ass woman that you are. She may not like it, but she'll have to respect it. If you can, concede to meet for coffee with her. After all, she's your mother, and you'll need coffee anyway.

Saying "No" to Requests from Super Women in Training

You can be a Super Woman *and* a Woman's Woman. I am. I love paying it forward to up-and-coming Super Women. But, if I said "yes" to all the inbound inquiries of women hoping for mentor advice, I wouldn't be able to do my own job. I try to be thoughtful about helping those who have really put, well, thought into their requests. But, even then, you can still say "no" the right way:

Your mentee: "Hi, Nicole! I'm applying for that new job I was telling you about and would love to meet up this week to go through my resume together. When are you free?"

You: "Hi there! I'm so glad you're going for it and applying for this job! I don't have time to meet up in person this week, but would be happy to offer a few notes over email. Can you send me your latest resume and cover letter?"

Your mentee: "Sure, I'm sending it right now!"

You: "Great! Let's reconnect at The Coffee Shop next Wednesday at 5 PM to talk through a few interview questions. I know you're going to nail it."

Your mentee: "Perfect, see you then!"

Why this works:

- Obviously, it takes a lot more time to meet in person than to tackle something remotely. I'm all about meeting (wo)mano-a-(wo)mano when you can, but if you don't have time and the ask is something document related like this, you can be just as helpful remotely. Cue: Track Changes.
- Notice that I asked her for her resume *and* cover letter. I knew she'd end up asking for my help on both eventually, and by anticipating that ahead of time, I reduced the need for back-and-forth emails—and saved myself more time, like a boss. Of course, only anticipate the additional ask if you have time to follow through.

- If you *do* have time to meet up in person, offer up a specific time and place. This reduces the back-and-forth while also drawing specific boundaries around your time.

KEEP IT TIGHT, KEEP IT RIGHT

When you're trying to say "no" to someone, especially over email, it's easy to turn into Emily Brontë and spew out a bunch of flowery prose in order to let them down easy. Don't get me wrong; I love me some Brontë. But there is a time and place for it, and it's not in boundary-defining conversations—it makes it too hard to decipher what the heck you are trying to say.

Cut the keyboard diarrhea by:

1. Using active voice (I *can* or I *can't* instead of I *would* or I *might*)
2. Cutting down on adverbs and adjectives (including "very," "so," and the overused "hectic")
3. Following the "Five Sentence Rule" by keeping all of your emails to five sentences or fewer (more than that, go for a phone call or actual meeting)

I know it's scary to hold back all of your warmth, excitement, and apologies over email. But, get to the point, even if the point is a big ol' N-O. Oftentimes, saying less will yield you more: sanity, respect, and time.

> There's nothing to apologize for when you're practicing the power of politely saying "no." And to make sure you don't, there is an email plug-in you can download called "Just Not Sorry," which alerts you to words or phrases that may undermine your messaging. Use it, and save the "Sorry" for real, in-person fuckups.
>
> **FYI**

In *Dirty Dancing*, Baby goes from a shy, awkward girl who lets her family dictate her life to a badass dancing babe who finally has the nerve to stand up to her family and go after the life *she* wants. How did she do it? In short, Baby got some boundaries.

Take a page from that script. I did. Eventually, I learned how to establish boundaries for myself despite my workaholic, people-pleasing tendencies. Only once I boldly protected my personal space and time from anyone trying to dictate it could I fully pursue the life *I* wanted.

Remember: Nobody puts a Super Woman in the corner.

BOTTOM LINE

Conventional Wisdom: I have to run full speed ahead in order to break the glass ceiling.

Nope. Knowing how and why to pace yourself is the number-one skill of Olympic track stars *and* C-suite executives. If you don't set boundaries around your domain, which includes your time, your energy, and even your feelings, people can and will take advantage of you. As many of the greatest female leaders out there will tell you, sometimes breaking that glass ceiling requires putting up some scaffolding first.

Conventional Wisdom: Saying "no" disappoints people.

Just like establishing boundaries is a sign of strength, so is having the moxie to say "no" to anything you're not more than jazzed about. Start looking at saying "no" as a courtesy to the asker. A sincere, well-stated "no" tells others you value *their* time. There's no better way to break trust than by committing to something, only to drop the ball later.

Conventional Wisdom: I need to be a "yes" woman in order to have a successful career.

You already know that your time is valuable, but articulating it reminds those around you just how valuable it is, too. Even if the ask is coming from your boss, you maintain the right to request an extended deadline or additional resources in order to set yourself up for success (and a good manager will recognize that). Don't forget that your time to build a legacy in life is limited. Protect that shit fiercely.

6

HACKING PRODUCTIVITY

Work Less, Do More

Work *smarter*, not *harder*. Yeah, yeah, we've heard that a million times. The idea sounds terrific, in theory—but WTF does "smarter" actually mean? I can tell you that none of my degrees or certifications made me, well, smart enough to figure it out. That is, until I got schooled by my breakdown and had to find a way to make my work *work* for me.

I've since learned that "working harder" means having a calendar full of back-to-back meetings but not actually getting much done. That's being *busy*. On the other hand, "working smarter" means being thoughtful and efficient about scheduling. That's being *productive*.

If you look up the word "busy" in a thesaurus, you'll find that its origins are "anxious" and "occupied." However, "productive" has synonyms like "energetic" and "rewarding." Being "busy" isn't the way to reach the goals you set back in Step 3. Being "productive," however, is what will allow you to sustain yourself and your schedule so that you can actually achieve those goals. In this step we are going to put your goals and your schedule together, helping you work *smarter* once and for all.

WORK IT

The traditional workweek is five days; we know that. But do you know how many of those days are actually productive workdays? Just *two*.

Researchers surveyed people who work a traditional forty-hour workweek on how many of those hours they consider productive, and the average was sixteen hours. Now, for a society that bemoans working so much and having poor so-called "work/life" balance because of it, how are we wasting twenty-nine whole hours of productivity every single week?

THE DOS AND DON'TS OF PRODUCTIVE PEOPLE

I've interviewed hundreds if not thousands of very productive people, and I can tell you that they are not magically productive; they have systems they have perfected over the years to work like magic for them. Super Woman Cathy Engelbert, who is the CEO of Deloitte, with 80,000 employees reporting to her, grew up a college athlete with five brothers and two sisters. She says she is competitive about almost everything. "I've learned that productivity should not be a competitive sport; you're never going to win." Over time, you'll develop your own productivity hacks and ways to shore up lagging motivation, but here are a few of my field-tested dos and don'ts to get you started:

- *Don't* forget about the boundaries you set in the last step and cancel personal plans because you feel like you are "too busy" to work out or see a friend.

- *Do* determine whether holding the meeting in person is something you need to do, or whether it would be more time effective on Skype (sans travel time). If it does need to be in person, try a "standing meeting" (yes, like one where you actually stand your ass up); they tend to be more productive.

- *Don't* schedule something for thirty minutes or an hour just because that looks organized on your calendar. If a meeting should only take seven minutes, then great, the meeting can be over and you just got twenty-three minutes of your valuable time back. There's no need to chitchat until the end of the allotted time; it probably should have been scheduled for only fifteen minutes to begin with.

- *Do* streamline your choices for basic stuff like food and clothes throughout the day. It's no coincidence that Steve Jobs had a "uniform" of jeans and a black turtleneck. Simon Cowell and Mark Cuban have been known for this, too. Think that's only a guy thing? Nope. The uber-Super Woman Jenna Lyons (who transformed J.Crew into the megabrand it is today) minimizes her wardrobe staples so that she can just reach into her closet and know she'll pull out a winner. Having to make fewer mundane choices throughout the day leaves more time for making the important ones.

- *Don't* ignore your body clock and how you feel at different times of the day. Take your natural rhythms into consideration when planning your schedule. Within the first two to four hours of waking up, your brain is the sharpest it's going to be all day, and research shows that the afternoon, specifically 3 PM, is the most optimal time for social activities, like meetings. Your body is on your side; trust that bitch.

- *Do* utilize communication apps like Slack or One-Note, but only if you actually like using them. The founder and CEO of Bumble, Whitney Wolfe Herd, has her employees use Facebook Messenger, under the theory that "everyone is super comfortable with it because they've been using it personally" so they are more likely to be productive with it.

Of course, there are days when your big-girl productivity pants aren't gonna fit no matter how hard you try to squeeze your ass into them. Shit happens. There are emergencies. Disasters. Breakups. Days when you can barely function at all, much less be "productive." I get that. I've had days that don't start with a gratitude journal entry, that find all my "nonnegotiables" becoming "not doables." It's okay. Remember: Superwoman is the one who tries to be perfect. Super Women know that over time, even small things can make a big difference. A mosquito can give you malaria. A butterfly can change the weather. And, you can take baby steps all the way to the finish line.

THREE TOP TIME-MANAGEMENT TRICKS FROM FELLOW SUPER WOMEN

Melinda Gates, cofounder of the Bill & Melinda Gates Foundation, which tackles some of the world's most pressing issues like polio and reproductive health, often talks about curbing burnout by taking fifteen minutes throughout the day to fill what she calls her own "joy bucket." She says that, in order to be good at her work, she needs quiet time to close out one meeting before she heads into the next. "I'm a big believer in taking time to pause and reflect," she says, "particularly when you're working on some of the big challenges in the world."

Rashida Jones, the actress known for playing Ann Perkins on *Parks and Recreation*, practices a no-phones-for-an-hour rule with her writing partner, Will McCormack, when they're trying to get work done. "It seems utterly ridiculous that two grown-ups wouldn't be able to stay away from their phones for just an hour, but there are many days when my phone owns me. And the rule helps," she says.

Emily Weiss, founder of Glossier, has mastered her own internal clock to know when she is the most productive, and she targets those times of day accordingly. "Definitely not mornings, I'm NOT a morning person," she says. "I would say

[I'm best] in the afternoons. I do work on the sofa or out on the deck." She is also known to hold meetings outside. "I like not sitting at a desk, and I move around a lot."

SCHEDULE DOWN

After fifteen years of nonstop hustling, I crashed. I'd heard of people with hardcore, stressful careers—like mine—having breakdowns. But I never thought one of those people would be *me*. I thought I was tougher than that. Stronger than that. Until I *was* one of those people, and I had no choice but to rethink . . . everything.

A major (and majorly overdue) overhaul was my daily schedule. Right up until I ended up on someone else's watch in the hospital, my schedule had been ridiculously unsustainable. But that's the way I'd wanted it to be.

When I set out to start my own company in 2011, I had two major goals in mind: 1) to produce smart, engaging content on financial topics that a younger generation of (mostly) women could relate to, and 2) to hire a killer team of (mostly) women who not only always had my best interests in mind, but were also just as ambitious and smart as I was, if not more so. I (mostly) succeeded on both accounts.

I had just turned twenty-seven when I started my company, and my future burnout and subsequent breakdown wasn't remotely on my radar. I couldn't even comprehend them as possibilities. It was full speed ahead, baby. Business bossdom or bust.

I have never been a *Devil Wears Prada*–type boss, but from

the beginning, I was strict about wanting to be scheduled up to the minute. My team worked their booties off to make sure I was, indeed, overbooked the way I wanted, even though I know they often questioned the value in it, and, after all, were the ones who had to deal with the sometimes-ugly ramifications of that schedule—like me getting sick because I was running myself down and then having to reschedule everything as a result. (Not to mention, the days when I was just plain exhausted and a cranky lady to be around.)

I just went where my calendar told me to go, and I wanted that calendar to be full, from a breakfast meeting to start the day to another one for drinks at its close. The more jam-packed my day, the more I felt like I was accomplishing, and the happier I thought I was. When I traveled and found myself with even a thirty-minute break, I was not happy. When I wasn't on the optimal flights for defying the space-time continuum (like red-eyes and super early departures between NYC and LA), I was not happy. When I had basically any free time at all, I was not happy.

Working harder, being "busier" than everyone else seemed like the only way to succeed. I imagined myself as the most conditioned athlete on the field, with more of a chance to win than those less used to a frantic pace. Living in a state of breathlessness was how I felt most comfortable and secure. I was running fast and hard to get "there," to "success," where I thought I would be happy. And if the way to get "there" was to grind, I would grind myself into the ground.

And, I did. I barely left time to shower and was running on at least two venti Americanos a day and little else. I was no longer just running but running *out*—of breath and fuel. And the pace wore on me not only physically, but mentally; I couldn't think straight anymore. I didn't stop to gain perspective on what I was doing, whom I was meeting with, and *why*, because I was always trying to get to the next thing on my schedule. I wasn't busy with purpose, I was just . . . busy and on the doorstep of burnout. My shrink would tell you that I was running from my PTSD diagnosis and distracting myself with work. Well, guess what? My shrink is a shrink because she knows a lot about this stuff. And she was right, as she often is, even though I'm always telling her, "Don't go all Freudian on me and psychoanalyze everything." She laughs and does it anyway, which I appreciate—well, eventually.

To reset after things fell apart, I ran away (briefly) not to distract myself from, but to confront, what went wrong. I peaced out to the most peaceful place I could find outside the city. I told the team to put a pause on scheduling (they looked at me like I had three heads and probably thought, "Who are you and what have you done with Nicole?") until I came back to them with more direction. As much as I loved and trusted my work squad, relinquishing total control of my time and not paying attention to where I was going until I was in a car or on a plane on the way there wasn't going to work anymore.

CONFESSIONS
OF A SUPER WOMAN

I'll Never Forget My First

. . . "mental health day." I had heard of this magical thing, but it wasn't something I had ever tried before. I drove out of the city and went on a hike in the Catskills. Yes, like on a school day. I had never been to the Catskills—or anywhere in the state outside of New York City. I had actually been to very few places "just because."

When I arrived, the nice lady in the tourism office gave me a map. Apparently, just to get to the trailhead to start my hike, I had to first take a "picturesque" mile-long trail. Ugh. My penchant for maximum efficiency was already being put to the test.

"It's so beautiful, it's almost meditative," she assured me. "It's down an old rail track."

Another ugh. I hated meditation. But, "Okay," I said. "All aboard!" (No one found that funny but me.)

"Picturesque" didn't do the trail justice. The old wooden tracks looked like the world's tallest ladder had lain flat on its back, looking up at a canopy of trees whose leaves had just started changing into a million brilliant shades of orange. The sun was out, but inside the tunnel of forest that enclosed the railroad track, it was cool, fresh, and dewy.

No one was on the trail as far ahead as I could see, and no one followed me. I started walking awkwardly on the uneven planks. To find my stride, I tried to focus only on the track beneath me. When I felt my mind drifting off to my calendar or my to-do list, I would force my focus back to the tracks. One step and then the next. One foot, then the other. Repeat.

Ohhhhh, I get it. I guess you don't have to be in a yoga studio saying "om" to meditate, I thought to myself.

I didn't think I was going to see anyone along my journey, but around the halfway mark, I heard a giggle. And it grew closer. I looked back and saw a bubbly little girl atop the shoulders of a man who looked to be a little younger than me. He was running down the tracks, off into the woods, and back onto the tracks, which seemed impossible considering how much trouble I was having just walking slowly along them on my own.

As they approached, I said, "Well, hello there! How do you do all that running and jumping on this trail?" I could barely walk on it.

Before her dad could say a word, the little girl replied, "We do this all the time when I'm at his house." She pointed down at his head from above it.

"That's so great! This is my first time; I live in the city. Where do you live?"

"I live right around here, sometimes, but I live at my mom's house, too, other times," said the girl, in this matter-of-fact way that made me feel like she was probably going to be a Supreme Court justice when she grew up.

"Ah—well, that's pretty cool that you have two houses," I said, trying to keep it light, as a child of divorce myself.

"Well, yes," her dad replied to her, looking uncomfortable and glancing at me. "For a while at least, while we work out our issues."

"Yeah, a lot of issues," the girl said without a hint of awkwardness, as basically the most grown-up of the three of us.

"What's your name, missy?" I asked, looking up at her.

"I'm Cadence," she said with confidence. "And I'm this many." She held up an open palm to show me five fingers.

And then with a wave, they were off down the trail, bobbing and weaving their way on and off the tracks together.

It was a five-minute conversation with a five-year-old. But it made me think: If this little girl has issues, then we *all* have issues. And her name was Cadence. Because of *course* it was. Cadence. Exactly what I needed.

Until this point I had bought into the stigma that "mental health" days are just an excuse to skip work and slack off. (Same? We'll get into the physical and financial benefits of mental health days in even greater detail in Step 11.) But somewhere in the middle of my first one (and the woods), I figured out what I'd been missing: my cadence, or a greater sense of my internal rhythm. With that in mind, I drove back into the city feeling rejuvenated and ready to develop, and stick to, a totally new type of schedule. Here's what I came up with:

NICOLE'S WEEKDAY PLAN (with variations depending on travel, events, speaking or press obligations, health, etc.)	
7 AM	Wake up
7 to 8 AM	Morning routine
8 to 9 AM	Cardio workout class 3x week and gym/weights or rest 2x week
9 to 10 AM	Get ready
10 to 10:30 AM	Respond to email
11 AM to 12:30 PM	Available to schedule a meeting, conference, or Skype call
12:30 to 1:30 PM	Lunch
1:30 to 2 PM	- Decide on social posts and website content for the day and pass on to my social media manager along with direction for engagement - Go over any important viewer or reader comments and emails I need to review
2 to 2:30 PM	- Research fun adventures/classes, book them, and put them in the calendar - Deal with any upcoming travel needs
2:30 to 3:30 PM	Shoot video or write (weekly or long-lead pieces, responses to interview requests, or some of my next book)
3:30 to 4 PM	Deal with logistical stuff—call accountant, schedule medical appointments, etc.
4 to 4:30 PM	Check email and follow up on any urgent happenings of the day—a new deal, progress of a project, direction for the team (if something really, really urgent came up, that person would know how to get ahold of me, like on the phone)
5:30 to 6 PM	Catch up on personal texts and calls
6 to 8 PM	- Attend a fun one-off class (anything from DJing to BYOB painting) - Take a regular course one day/week to build mastery in something and develop a regular community (first one is a six-week-long improv class on Mondays)
8 to 9:30 PM	Dinner date: with myself, a guy, or a friend
9:30 to 11 PM	Nighttime routine and goal setting
11 PM	Lights out

My weekend schedule was sure to look a little different, but I planned to keep some of these elements consistent throughout, like my morning and nighttime routine (outlined in detail in the next step). But on both weekdays and weekends, there is one crucial element of my new marching orders that doesn't show up on my rundown above: flexibility. Because, while I get that this *looks* like the schedule of a marine, I vowed not to be super militant. After all, keeping myself to an overly rigid schedule is what had gotten me in trouble in the first place. But as the weeks went on, I found that the closer I kept to this new schedule, the better I felt. I was way more productive, and being more *productive*—not just mindlessly *busy*, mind you, but mindfully getting shit done—made me feel laser focused and more in control.

> A Harvard study found that we only pay attention to what we are doing 47 percent of the time. More than half our time is spent not even paying attention to what we are paying attention to.

FYI

Balance is as much about managing your attention as it is about managing your day. Creating a strong outline for a sustainable schedule not only allowed me to catch my breath, it also ensured that I was aware of how and where I was allocating my time. I didn't need to hike the Appalachian Trail to find what I'd been looking for, just to walk (well, stumble) along a bunch of railroad tracks. It was order in chaos. A consciousness. A cadence.

FIND YOUR CADENCE

Remember: you are not something broken that needs to be "fixed," but hey, even a baby grand needs a little fine-tuning. So make an outline of your own schedule. Feel free to take inspiration from mine, keeping in mind that everyone's ideal day will look different depending on your priorities, commitments, work schedule, and commute. Then take a peek under the lid of the piano. What's in there? What's working? What's not? Working "smarter" doesn't require the smarts you learned in school. It's something you can teach yourself anytime. Hint: it's *now o'clock*.

For Super Women who freelance or work for themselves, a general outline of your daily plan is useful because it adds structure to an otherwise free-flowing day. But it can also be super helpful in making sure you have enough in your "joy bucket." Are you scheduling lunch and coffee meetings for every single break of the week? Well, take those breaks back! Limit yourself to two lunches and two coffee dates in any given week, so that you can use the rest of your break time to regroup on your own—whether that's eating your lunch outside, going to the gym, making a personal phone call, or anything else that brings you "joy."

I get that some of your workday is dictated by others (i.e., your boss and clients) and those commitments likely can't be tinkered with. But you can and should make more conscientious choices about how you spend the time you can tinker with. For example, be very aware of the calendar invitations that you accept. If it's from your boss? Yep, you probably have to go. But if it's a group meeting that you could easily digest in note form later on from one of your colleagues, decline. Others will come to value your time only if you value it first.

Play Hard to Get

People often say to me now, "You're so hard to get ahold of!" like somehow that's a bad thing. Well, if I'd been too frazzled to remember to get back to that person, then maybe it would be. On the other hand, if I made a conscious decision to respond at my own time, then I'd take that remark as a compliment. And I do. I respond at 10 AM or 4 PM, as you can see from my schedule.

Come up with two or three blocks of time that work best for you. Otherwise, responding to emails and texts as soon as they come in pulls you away from whatever you are doing and lets other people determine the course of your day. You don't wake up thinking, "Today, I'm just gonna wing it!" So, why would you relinquish control of your time, one of your most important superpowers, by feeling compelled to respond to messages the second they come in? That's letting someone hijack your time little by little until your whole day is in their hands—and not in yours where it belongs.

As former Yahoo CEO Marissa Mayer said, "burnout is about resentment, [and preventing it] is about knowing yourself well enough to know what it is you're giving up that makes you resentful." So, identify the thing that, if you missed it, would make you resentful at your work, whether it's distraction-free date night on Fridays or Sunday brunch with the besties. Then, it's up to you to schedule and take your own "PTO." In this case, it doesn't stand for "Paid Time Off" but rather "Predictable Time Off." Workplace studies have shown that the predictability of "me time" is more beneficial to overall productivity than the duration of it. Because of that, companies are implementing predictable policies and rules like "no email before 6 AM and after 8 PM" or "call on the weekend, but only if it's urgent." Create your own parameters—that you can count on and look forward to—for your "PTO" because, after all, no matter where you work or whom you might work for, *you* are always the boss of you.

FILL IN THE BLANKS

The rough outline of your day probably has a lot of blanks like mine does. For example, my schedule outline has things like "shoot video or write" and "deal with logistical stuff." You might have things like "outline notes before performance review" and "organize household paperwork." Every day, you need to determine what, specifically, goes into those categories. There's a lot that *could* fit—practice asking for the raise you deserve or track down and print out all positive feedback you've received from others, in the former example, or decide whether you're going to tackle monthly bills or file your taxes for the latter—but the best fits are the tasks that, you guessed it, move you toward accomplishing your goals.

"But there's wayyyyy too much I need to do today—I'll never be able to fit it all in, much less think about goals, Lapin!" Oh yeah? What exactly do you *need* to do today?

I have a daily exercise to help figure that out. At the outset, I know it looks like I'm adding *yet another* to-do to your already-packed day, but like the gratitude journal we talked about in Step 2, I promise the time investment is worth it. You can do this just in an ordinary notebook, several little notebooks like fitness entrepreneur Tracy Anderson does, or you can use *The Super Woman Journal*. Here's what you need to establish:

1. *What's already scheduled today*. Identify everything nonnegotiable already on your calendar. This includes your commute, important meetings, and family commitments, like picking up your kid from day care.

2. *What I could do*. Brain dump all the things you can possibly think of that could work for the "fill in the blanks." This includes the specific tasks within each area. So the "outline notes" slot would have things like determining your plan of attack for asking for a raise and tracking down and printing out all the positive feedback you've received, as mentioned previously.

3. *What fits with my goals*. Look at what you wrote for your four Fs. Eliminate or "procrastinate" (I'll tell you how to strategically do that next) whatever is not super time sensitive in your brain dump. Then,

which of the things remaining align with your goals? Rank those in descending order of priority. Start with number one—aka, it *must* get done today—and save the items you don't get to for another day.

Eat the Frog

SUPER WOMAN TIP

Mark Twain said, "If it's your job to eat a frog, it's best to do it first thing in the morning. And if it's your job to eat two frogs, it's best to eat the biggest one first."

Now, I'm not suggesting that you eat an actual frog. But I *am* suggesting that you get the most difficult task of the day done first. If you have to fire someone, take accountability for something, tackle an intimidating project, then do it—first. Get it over with. Putting off and stressing about the thing you're dreading only gives it more of your brain's real estate. That's valuable headspace you can fill with the rest of the items on your to-do list once it's done.

"Busy" people fill in their schedule indiscriminately: organizing your desktop, picking up dry-cleaning, and grabbing drinks with an acquaintance whom you have no real interest in seeing are all examples of this. "Productive" Super Women prioritize their tasks in accordance with their goals and Emotional Wellness needs: nailing a major deadline at work, attending your favorite workout class, and checking in with a close friend who is going through a tough time are examples of this. We pay close attention to what we do with our day and put thoughtful intention into how we fill in our schedule.

PROCRASTINATION TRANSFORMATION

I have two favorite quotes about procrastination. The first is from Thomas Jefferson: "Never put off till tomorrow what can be done today." And the other is another from our frog-eating friend Mark Twain: "Never put off till tomorrow what you can do the day after tomorrow."

I love the first quote, but I live for the second. Contrary to what we've been taught to believe, procrastination isn't always a bad thing. Yep, you heard it here first: procrastination can be *good* if, and only if, you're thoughtful about it. The word derives from the Latin "*pro*" which means "forward," and "*crastinus*" which means "belonging to tomorrow." So, if something belongs to tomorrow and you are planning for it as you would anything else, there's no need to beat yourself up for letting it actually belong to tomorrow and not today.

Creating a productive plan for the day is all about prioritizing *today*, which necessarily means putting some things off until tomorrow or later. Procrastinating in this mindful, intentional manner will help you in two ways: 1) it will keep you from slicing your time too thinly, and 2) it will protect more urgent tasks from suffering because your attention gets diverted by something less urgent that pops up in your in-box, which can be done tomorrow. Some say procrastination is the thief of productivity. I say that if it's done strategically, it can actually be productivity's heroine.

Think about how your daily tasks support or detract from moving your goals forward. It's only when you keep those in mind that you can prioritize accordingly. I'll walk you through an example of how to connect the dots between the two. Let's say your goals for this year are:

1. Leave your job
2. Start a chocolate shop
3. Find true love
4. Get buns of steel

And your potential tasks for today are:

1. Pick up dry-cleaning
2. Meet with a cocoa supplier in your area
3. Go to a bar with your friends
4. Go to a luncheon at work for a new committee

First of all, I like most of the goals you are throwing down. I like that you want to "find true love" instead of "get married and have kids"—keeping it realistic given the year time frame. Similarly, you're working to "get buns of steel," not "become a size four"—getting in shape to be healthy, not to conform to some misguided size goal. As for leaving your job to start a chocolate shop, I'm intrigued by the idea (who doesn't love chocolate and a Boss Bitch?), but you might need to scale back a bit for the year-long time frame we're working with.

Especially at the beginning of each year, we tend to go balls to the wall with lofty pronouncements about what we will get done in the next 365 days. Resolutions can be helpful in jump-starting your ambitions, but it's smart to procrastinate on some of those goals as well. It's better to have something as part of your three- or five-year plan than to put it on the list for year one and then feel disappointed when you don't achieve it because you were overshooting by putting it there in the first place.

As I wrote in *Boss Bitch*, when starting your own business, it's important to have your next move lined up, as well as a solid cushion of savings before you burn that corporate bra. Hey, if you can make all that happen in a few months, go you! But, if you want to make those chocolate shop dreams a reality, I would suggest setting more realistic goals for this year, like "Make sure my business plan is airtight," "scale back expenses so that I have nine months of living expenses in the bank," and "find an independent health-care option for when I leave my corporate job and lose my benefits." These smaller, actionable goals will keep you on track toward achieving the big one of leaving your job altogether. Plus, it will feel motivating to cross them off your list in, say, years one and three, so that by the time you get to year five, you're ready to start making it rain (chocolate).

Now, on to your tasks. Let's say they are:

1. *Pick up dry-cleaning.* Unless you have no clothes left in your closet, which I find hard to believe, then dry-cleaning can wait.

2. *Meet with a cocoa supplier in your area.* Meeting with resources and gathering recon toward starting your business is very important, especially if you want to get it off the ground quickly. Do this.

3. *Go to a bar with your friends.* Yes. If your goal is to find true love, dating apps are all well and good, but meeting someone the old-fashioned way is better, especially with a squad of wingwomen.

4. *Go to a luncheon at work for a new committee.* If you're planning to leave your job, there's no need to waste time taking on additional responsibilities at the office. Veto.

If we connect the dots: Task 2 goes with Goal 2. Task 3 goes with Goal 3. And Tasks 1 and 4 aren't related to your goals.

So, if you skip Task 1, did you "procrastinate" on picking up your dry-cleaning? Yes. Does that mean you have more time to get ready for the bar and drive to and from the cocoa supplier? Yes—and *that's* more important to advancing your long-term goals of finding a partner and starting your own business. If you skip Task 4, did you decline joining another committee, which a) you don't have time for, and b) won't advance you toward your goal of starting your own thing? Yes. And that means you have more time to get ready to go out shopping for love at the bar, which *is* a goal of yours.

Crossing everything off your list might feel satisfying and might make Mr. Thomas Jefferson proud, but you'd be letting yourself down in the future—and for what, a few more cathartic checks on a to-do list? Truly working *smarter* means putting off what can be done tomorrow or even the next day and focusing instead on the quality, not quantity, of tasks you prioritize today. It's the only way to work less and win more in the long run.

CONFESSIONS
OF A SUPER WOMAN

I'm Basically Miss America

Well, minus the tiara. But hear me out.

This might surprise you, but I was one of the judges in the 2016 Miss America pageant. It's something I always wanted to do; I wanted a voice in determining which young woman would represent her peers over the next year. The Miss America Organization is the largest scholarship organization in the country for women. In the pageant world, Miss America is considered to be *the* one for smart, wholesome young women . . . I mean, Diane Sawyer, the ultimate Super Woman, was a junior Miss America before she went on to the White House and network news superstardom.

When I started my judging orientation before the pageant got underway, I was told that we wouldn't be looking for the prettiest, smartest, or most talented woman on the stage. *Wait, what?!*

The president of the organization explained, "She's Miss America: consistently good across the board."

He was, obviously, right. The Miss America pageant uses Olympic-style scoring. The contestants' top scores in each category are thrown out, and the category scores are averaged into an overall score. The finalists didn't necessarily get 10s, but they got high enough marks in every category to move on to the finals.

The judges couldn't talk to each other until after the judging was over but, of course, we all had our "favorites," and after we did talk, I realized that the women in the final round weren't the other judges' number-one picks in any given category either. But when the finalists were announced, we all kinda felt like, "Oh, yeah, she was great."

The young women who did the best didn't work too hard at one thing. That wasn't going to get them the crown. Instead, the winners worked strategically with the amount of time they had to prepare. They used their minutes on the stage to go for high marks—but not necessarily the highest—in each category, and then quickly pivoted to the next one. They focused on an overall plan that would show the judges how strong they were across the board.

So, at the end of the competition, I told the president, "You know, you were wrong about something. The winner *is* the best at one thing. She's the best at working the *smartest*."

You might think, "I don't need a full-on plan for my waking hours, I have enough self-control to avoid getting sucked in or sidetracked by distractions." Well, to that I say: The most savvy people I know make a thoughtful outline for their day by connecting the dots of their tasks to their goals, then plan accordingly. That's how they actually achieve said goals. (BTW:

the winner of Miss America the year I judged was named Savvy . . . seriously.)

Trying to ace everything all the time is *hard* on yourself, and difficult to sustain—and that doesn't even mean you come out a winner. The *smart* way to ensure victory is to keep your eyes on the crown (your goals). It's time to hang up your "busy badge of honor" for good and step out with your new "productive badge of honor." I know you'll rock it. And I'm sure the judges will agree.

BOTTOM LINE

Conventional Wisdom: My day is dictated by what's in my inbox each morning; I have to respond to those emails before I do anything else.

Your day, your week, your life is dictated by *you*. You are the author. So start each day with in-tention, not in-box. You're in charge of each day's narrative, because you're the one writing it. And if you don't like where you are, it's a safe bet that what got you here won't get you where you want to go.

Conventional Wisdom: My life is too chaotic to have a set schedule.

If you want to make the most of each day, you first need to know (at least roughly) what the cadence of your day is going to look like. Of course, stuff comes up, and your weekday schedule, like mine, changes a lot. But giving yourself a foundation, any foundation, on which to construct your priorities for the day will only keep you building a more productive life. You can't control the chaos (we all have our own version of it), but you can control your response to it.

Conventional Wisdom: Winners are the best at everything.

No way, no how. In life, and in the Miss America pageant as I discovered, the winner is the best at managing her time and skill set, finding the most efficient way to get to the goal. And there she is, Miss Productive.

STEP

7

PUT DOWN THE F-ING PHONE

Go on a Digital Detox

Once you're done checking your phone for the millionth time today (I'll wait . . .), I'd love to get on with this book. You're officially past the halfway mark, and well on your way to becoming a Super Woman. Now let's get a handle on how much time you spend on your phone—because nothing will give your Emotional Wellness an immediate boost like powering down (or damage it by not).

Does the idea of putting your phone away make your palms sweat? If so, that's okay: Head back to Step 1 for a bit to admit you have a problem, and it's a phone addiction. Most of us have one (I sure did!). And it's easy to see why: mobile devices have replaced our calendars, our cameras, our calculators, and pretty much every other helpful tool that used to operate on its own.

The average adult touches her or his phone eighty times per day. I can't think of anything else you do voluntarily eighty times per day. Not eat. Not hug. Not even smile (the average number of smiles per day for adults is twenty). In this step, I'm going to teach you how to make sure your phone doesn't replace your life—and sabotage your career.

Before we get started, here's a challenge for you: Check your phone now, one last time, and don't check it again until you've finished this step. I won't say "don't check it at all for the rest of the book" because then you'll just put *me* away. I'll give you one last peek just to make sure you didn't miss anything major, and, in return, you'll give me 28 pages of your tech-free attention. Deal? Deal.

WHO IS IN CONTROL OF YOUR LIFE . . . YOU OR YOUR SMARTPHONE?

We've worked so hard up to this point to draw boundaries and make plans so that no one controls you or your time but you. But we've all gotten into pretty serious, often controlling relationships with our devices. Would you ever let another person control you or your time like they do? No. So let's cut the cord on their control, too.

CONFESSIONS
OF A SUPER WOMAN

The Road to Tech Hell Is Paved with Good Intentions

I had just started my job anchoring a business show on Bloomberg, and I immediately set off planning segments and booking guests. In news (and life in general), it's all about relationships, so I needed to dig in right away to prepare for going on the air two weeks later.

I was relentless in my mission to find the best interviews for the show. The show's focus was technology and new media, so I made a list of every public tech company (from Apple to Qualcomm) and every unicorn (private companies worth $1 billion or more). I listed their founders and CEOs in a spreadsheet and committed to keeping at it until *every single one of them* was booked on the show. I became a smartphone machine, on my phone talking and emailing all day long. In other words, I was exactly the breathless, unbalanced woman I've been talking about not being throughout this book.

A few days before we started, my boss (who had recruited me for this position and really wanted me to succeed) set up a video conference with the rest of the team in San Francisco.

"Thank you so much for being on the call, guys," he said, as he introduced me to the team.

"Yeah, I'm so thrilled that I've already gotten going," I said, scrolling through my phone with one hand.

"We are, too," said my colleague on the other line, "and here's what we are thinking and how we work." I began frantically typing an email on my phone. I'm sure I did have some actual messages to respond to. But I also wanted the team to see just how hard I was working and how seriously I was taking this job. "Blah blah does this and blah blah is where . . . ," I heard as I typed away.

Out of the corner of my eye, I saw my boss get on his phone. *See! We know what we need to do to get ahead. He gets me!* I thought.

. . . And just then, another email came through! I tapped on it immediately.

It was a one-line message—*from my boss*. "Pay attention, Lapin. Get off your phone."

Shit.

My intention wasn't to come across as a bad team player or disrespectful. Quite the contrary, I was working *for* the team—and wanted them to know it. But what I would come to realize is that working *for* the team and working *with* the team are two different things. Being distracted and unprofessional is only one of the ways your phone saps your superpowers. If you want others to value your valuable time, you must pay them the same respect. That means being present in meetings and actively listening to those around you—not mindlessly nodding over the top of your screen.

Funny enough, in that job at Bloomberg, I was anchoring a technology-focused show that reported a lot on how profitability drove our tech obsession. Much of the revenue generated by technology companies—from hardware makers to game developers to social networks—focuses on "eye time." So it's in the best interest of their bottom line to keep us hooked. And it's worked.

The average adult refreshes her or his phone 150 times per day. We are awake for an average of sixteen hours a day, so if you do the math, we are checking them every six and a half minutes. We look at our phone before our feet hit the floor. We look at it on the way to the bathroom. We look at it in the bathroom.

There's a spot-on cartoon that depicts a man walking into the gates of heaven where God says, "Actually, you had a pretty great life, but you were looking down at your phone and missed it." It's biting commentary but it's true. Our devices used to serve us. Now we serve our devices.

TALK SCIENCE TO ME

Let's talk about our big, beautiful brains. Now, obviously, I am no neuroscientist, but while researching for this book, I learned some pretty important things about how our brains work. And to understand why I am pushing you to unlatch the phone from your palm, we should get less heady and more brainy.

You might think that some of the advice I'm giving you to boost your Emotional Wellness is *fugazi* (origin unknown, but it basically means "fake"—and it's part of one of my favorite Matthew McConaughey lines in *The Wolf of Wall Street*: "Fugayzi, fugazi. It's a whazy. It's a woosie. It's fairy dust. It doesn't exist."). But it's all rooted in science. In fact, that's one of the reasons I decided to write this book in the first place: to explore what about Emotional Wellness is for real and what's, well, fugazi.

DOPAMINE IS DOPE

I'm sure you've heard of dopamine. You might think of it as the "happy juice" in your brain. We've long known that dopamine controls the pleasure systems of the brain, causing you to feel enjoyment from things like sex, drugs, food, and, yes, technology. That is true, but more recent research has revised our understanding of dopamine ever so slightly, but importantly. Dopamine is now believed to cause you to *want, seek,* and *search for* those things that make you happy. We now know that we gain pleasure through the *search* for enjoyment, not simply *having* it.

We've seen this play out in the online dating world: Despite 26 million matches made each day on Tinder alone, fewer than 10 percent of matches are consummated with an actual exchange; the rest of the time, users opt to keep swiping instead of messaging the matches they've already made. For the vast majority of users, the game itself proves to be more arousing than the other players. Case in point: nearly half of the millennials in this survey admitted to using dating apps as "ego-boosting procrastination" rather than to meet people.

Biochemically, we are becoming addicted to the search. It's easy to get into a dopamine-induced endless loop of seeking information. Do these scenarios sound familiar?

Scenario 1
Desire: You want to look up Coco Chanel's birthday.
Action: Google it.

Scenario 2
Desire: You want to see what your former boss is doing these days.
Action: Look her up on LinkedIn.

Scenario 3
Desire: You want to tell your friend that you ran into

your ex-boyfriend at Starbucks.

Action: Text her.

These seem like totally normal responses. They provide instant gratification. Chanel's birthday is August 19, 1883. Your former boss is unemployed (ouch). And your friend texts you back right away asking you for the lowdown on your ex.

But what happens next?

Scenario 1

Action 2: You start perusing Chanel's most famous quotes for use in future Instagram captions.

Scenario 2

Action 2: You start searching for where other people you've worked with in the past are now working.

Scenario 3

Action 2: You start gossiping about how your ex looked, what he was wearing, and whether or not he's seeing anyone.

Again, pretty normal sounding, right? But you just got yourself into a dopamine-technology cage match. The dopamine makes you start searching for what you want. You then get rewarded right away with what you want. So you search more to get more rewards. You go back and forth. You can't stop Googling, checking LinkedIn, and texting. Our dopamine receptors are never satiated; they keep saying, "gimme more, gimme more." So you keep searching long after you've found what you were looking for in the first place. You end up in a never-ending battle with your own brain.

THIS IS YOUR BRAIN ON TECHNOLOGY, ANY QUESTIONS?

Nomophobia. That's the actual real word for technology addiction or the fear of being off your phone. Might you have it?

I did. I used to be the woman who would boast about being on her phone 24/7/365. I remember saying to colleagues, "If I don't respond within three minutes, then I'm probably dead." But it is precisely because I was always available, and responded so often and so quickly for so many years, that I burnt out completely. The very thing I bragged about almost killed me. That joke about being dead is no longer funny to me.

Of course, technology isn't going anywhere—no one is going back to conducting business over snail mail any time soon—so we have to be able to use it but not abuse it, or let it abuse us. I can tell you anecdotally that my technology use played a big role in pushing me to my breaking point. But if my confessions and personal stories don't resonate with you, hey, that's cool, but the research should. Facts are facts, and not putting down your f-ing phone is just plain bad for you and your career. As if leaving a bad impression on those around you isn't enough, your phone addiction also affects the way your brain processes information—for the worse, stymieing your ability to handle new information as it comes in and limiting your capacity to retain that information for the long haul. Your brain is a living, evolving thing, which means that it's changing all the time. It's shaped by your daily life and experiences. And the word "shape," here, is not used in the "having influence" way, as in, "My grandma really shaped my views on politics." Nope. Your brain is actually *changing shape*. Here's how it plays out:

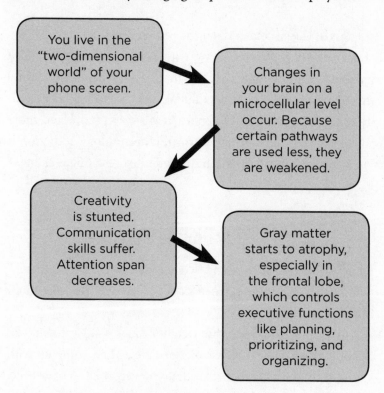

Conclusion 1: If a technology disorder can lead to poor executive functioning, and poor executive functioning means you have a hard time with work-critical skills like planning, prioritizing, and organization, then if you want to succeed at work . . . get off your f-ing phone.

Conclusion 2: If limiting technology use has been proven to positively affect Emotional Wellness by improving mood, relationships, and creativity, and Emotional

Wellness helps you succeed at work, then if you want to succeed at work . . . get off your f-ing phone.

Susan Greenfield, a scientific researcher in behavioral psychiatry at Oxford (who, along with being a total badass, also happens to be a baroness), warns that, as our daily lives are lived through smartphones, tablets, and laptops, we're losing our ability to connect with other people, resulting in more and more social isolation. In fact, she warns that technology addiction is "an issue as important and unprecedented as climate change." Preach, baroness, preach.

YOUR DIGITAL DIET

By now, you may be thinking: "Okay, okay, Lapin. I have a problem; I get it. No more science class . . . just tell me what to do to fix it."

If you were trying to lose weight or kick a sugar habit, you might start with a restricted diet or detox, then come up with a long-term maintenance plan that you can stick to over time. You can't—and shouldn't—eliminate fun from your life and live in austerity forever; you'll inevitably binge and return to old habits. To stick to your diet, you might treat yourself to a little piece of chocolate every night, so you don't end up chowing down on a huge hunk of chocolate cake and blowing all the hard work you've put in. When it comes to your digital life, the strategy is the same: we're going to start with a seven-day detox, then set up a realistic "technology plan" like you would a realistic "eating plan."

After all, technology can be a-mazing. It enables us to do things and connect with people in a way that's faster and easier than ever before. Who doesn't love catching up with family on the other side of the country over FaceTime or connecting with a friend over Words with Friends? But however a-mazing, it's just a tool. And just like any superpower, you can use it for good or you can use it for evil. Just make sure *you're* using *it*—not the other way around.

CONFESSIONS
OF A SUPER WOMAN

My Phone-Free Week

When people heard that *I* was going on a complete digital detox, many of them laughed and thought I was punking them. Of course, I was not. But, luckily, the people who supported me through it are the ones who matter to me; the ones who didn't, don't.

Knowing that I would never be able to fully disconnect if I remained in the city, with all of its easy distractions and endless barrage of screens, I opted for a full-on wilderness retreat. So there I was, in a cabin. With a shared bathroom. Basically glamping. With no phone. No emails to check. No texts. No camera. No apps. Nada. And even if I had managed to sneak in a phone, there was no cell service.

The first day was like coming off drugs—withdrawal to the max. Total separation anxiety. I was going on hikes with beautiful views that were just begging to be Instagrammed, and I had no way of even taking a photo. I was waiting in line for lunch with the other people on the retreat and had no phone to scroll idly through. I was alone in my room with books and paper, no social media to keep me company. And I was freaking the fuck out.

But each day, it got a little easier. And by the end, it was downright liberating. As I came down from my digital high, I observed some big changes in myself.

The first thing I noticed was that I was more conscious of the world around me, which I would have missed with a phone basically sutured to my hand. As I walked through the woods, I took in the various plants and shrubs and the differences in the texture of their leaves. I marveled at the different shades of wood in the paneling that lined my room. My senses were heightened in everything I did, from tying my shoes to watching a sunset that could only be captured with my eyes and memory.

The next thing I noticed was that I felt more alert at 6 AM than I usually did at 8 AM after two cups of coffee. Waking up to watch the sunrise was a) glorious and b) easy because I had less trouble falling asleep. There was no phone light beaming into my eyeballs before bed, ruining the natural darkness (and my eyes). Instead, I read, or simply fell right to sleep after a full, rich, adventurous day.

Finally, I noticed how present I was with everyone I talked to. I was more engaged in the stories they told. I remembered little details about each person I met and what we'd talked about in a way I never had before. I was even able to confront a few tough conversations, straight-on and in person (like with one, um, married guy who would not take a hint that

I was not interested in a romp in the woods), squashing conflict way faster than a barrage of texts would have.

Sure, these were all simple things I could have worked on before taking a digital time-out, but I never thought I needed to. I didn't even think to *think* about it. It took a week without my phone for me to really start looking outward at the world with fresh eyes and inward at the things about myself that I'd completely lost sight of.

YOUR SEVEN-DAY DIGITAL DETOX

A digital detox is a great way to jump-start your long-term digital plan. But you don't have to go on a dedicated digital detox program like I did to kick your habit; I'll give you a framework for a week-long boot camp you can put in place while still going to work, school, and just generally getting on with your everyday life.

Granted, any sort of boot camp or crash diet is not sustainable in the long run; the maintenance required to stay in the fabulous shape you've gotten yourself into is where the real work is. But old habits die hard, so let's kick your digital booty with a seven-day plan:

Day 1

Take little time-outs. Don't look at your phone for a time frame that includes two meals, either from breakfast through lunch or from lunch through dinner. For extra credit, turn it off completely. If you're traveling, on a juice cleanse, or anything else that messes with a regular meal schedule, then take four (consecutive) hours off your phone.

Day 2

Clean out the online riffraff. Go through the people you follow on Instagram and Twitter and remove anyone you aren't friends with anymore or don't have an interest in following. Apply the same principle that Marie Kondo talks about in her popular book, *The Life-Changing Magic of Tidying Up,* only this time for your online life instead of your home life: Anyone you follow must spark joy, or at least interest. Unfriend Facebook "friends" who aren't actually friends, and set your timeline settings to only see twenty or so people's updates at a time. (Like, seriously, do you really need to be wasting any brain cells on what your seventh-grade music teacher's daughter is eating for dinner? Um, no.)

Day 3

Master your settings. Go into the settings section of your phone and take control. First, turn off "video autoplay" so you only watch videos when you want to and don't get sucked into playlists or random videos you stumbled upon. Then, do an audit of the push notifications you have on your phone. Which do you really need? (I choose to receive only human notifications, like phone calls, and turn off any nonhuman notifications, like updates from apps or alerts from retailers.)

Do you *need* to know when Nordstrom is having an anniversary sale?

Do you *need* to know the very second someone comments on your photo?

Do you *need* to see every time someone on Tinder messages

you? (I know, you must be getting lots of messages. But remember, if you become *on* demand, you won't be *in* demand.)

Finally, do you *need* to know when everyone texts you in real time? I know, this one is the scariest of them all. But if you are bold enough, turn off text notifications. It's empowering as fuck to just look at texts when and only when you want to look at texts. If someone needs to get ahold of you for something legit, they will call you (yes, the phone works that way, too).

Day 4

Clear the app barnacles off your phone and untether from subscriptions. Honestly, this is gonna be a multiple-hour time investment—but it will save your sanity for much longer.

Step 1: Look at the apps you have. The average person has sixty to ninety apps on their phone but only uses *nine*. It's like your closet is stuffed with clothes, but you pretty much stick to two pairs of jeans, one hoodie, a black shirt, and yoga pants. To get a sense of your personal app usage, check the battery settings on your phone, which show the percentage of time you spend on each app. Keep those with crazy high percentages and delete the ones with little to no use. I'll bet you can delete about half of your apps right there. Now, look at the ones remaining. Has the app company shut down since you installed it? Did you only install the app to get a one-time discount? If so, delete.

Step 2: *Why* do you use them? Classify your apps into categories that don't sugarcoat what they are and how they are affecting you, and consider cutting some more loose. Researchers clump apps into these categories:

- **Apps that waste your time.** Remember that Bumble guy? Well, he's probably one of, what, fifteen Bumble guys you're talking to? Are you seriously going to meet all of them, or just have witty-ish chats that go on and on and on forever? If you're single, go ahead and get app-y, but get a grip on the time you spend on those dating apps. Try limiting yourself to just one app for a few weeks, and focus on developing a few good conversations with people you've actually matched with rather than "window shopping." The other big-time suckers are games like Candy Crush. Playing games is fun, I get it, but . . . get over it. The average person spends twenty-three days a year and almost four (!!) years of their lives looking at their smartphone. Do you really want to spend almost a month out of every year on Pokémon Go and Clash of Clans? Please say "no."

- **Apps that keep you on the clock 24/7.** Yes, yes, you're super-duper important. But do you really need a Google Drive app on your phone? Sure, writing a book on your phone *is* possible via Google Docs, but even as fast as you can text, I'll bet you can type faster. So, Ms. Austen, perhaps save your polished prose for proper computer time—or good ol' pen and paper.

- **Apps that may depress you.** Studies have shown that while social media might make you happy in the short term (by giving you that sweet hit of dopamine), it makes frequent users depressed in the long run, by contributing to low self-esteem. Think about what most of your friends are posting on social media: big

life updates, photos from their travel adventures, sel-
fies when they're in full makeup and have a million
filters at their disposal. It's a curated view of their
lives, not representative of who they *actually* are but
who they want to be perceived as, and geared toward
instant "liking" gratification. And, instead of avoiding this onslaught of staged fabulosity, research has
shown that teens with poor mental health are actually
greater users of social media, suggesting that they are
seeking out interactions in order to feel less crappy
and alone . . . which, in turn, only makes them feel
more crappy and alone. I'll be the first to say that it's
not just teens: in my less than super (adult) years, I
deleted photos that didn't get a lot of likes. WTF is
that all about? I was addicted to seeking admiration
and obsessing over if and when I got it while being
jealous of others who had more. That's not super—it's
lame. If you find you're comparing yourself to others
excessively, maybe it's time to delete.

Looking at your apps with these categories in mind, I hope
you deleted another half of those left.

Step 3: Take stock of which apps you pay a subscription for;
I'd bet there are quite a few on your phone that you don't even
know about. When you sign up for the "free trial," you probably
think, *yeah yeah, I'll delete it after a month and scam the system*.
Welp, the app companies bank on you forgetting to do just that,
and the system scams you, instead. Rethink the apps you are
paying for—how much are they really worth to you? (And don't
forget to cancel autopay for any apps you've already deleted in
the previous steps!)

In-Box Detox

SUPER WOMAN TIP

While you're app cleansing, hit your in-box as well. Unroll.Me pulls all of your email subscriptions into one list and then lets you check the ones you still want to get, versus the ones you want to kick out of your (newly organized) in-box. You can also adjust your Gmail settings to catch daily newsletters and push them into a special folder—this way, you can choose when to read them without losing them to spam. Just apply a filter looking for these oft-used phrases: "opt-out," "unsubscribe," "viewing the newsletter," "email notifications" or "update profile," and you'll catch 99 percent of the newsletters out there. Fewer daily emails means less need to compulsively refresh (plus fewer opportunities to get sucked into marketing ploys and makeup tutorials).

Step 4: Organize your remaining apps. Try to get them all onto the first screen; your phone will feel less cluttered and you'll spend less time swiping between screen pages. Divide them into buckets by category to get them all to fit on that first page. For instance, I have Delta and Hotels.com in my "travel" category and my bank, investment, and credit card apps under the "personal finance" category. There may be a few mandatory ones your phone manufacturer doesn't let you delete (see how they get ya!?), but the rest of the real estate is up to you.

Day 5

Leave your phone in another room to charge while you sleep.
Don't look at it for an hour before bed and for the first hour
after you wake up. We've already talked about it being a serious
knock on your productivity, but it is also detrimental to your
health. The blue light emitted from your cell phone screen is a
wavelength that boosts our attention, reaction times, and mood
during the day. But it has been shown to throw off your body's
natural melatonin levels, making it more difficult for you to fall
asleep at night, get that good REM sleep, and wake up rested
in the morning. So ban the blue around bedtime. (If you really
prefer to read on a device before bed, try the Kindle Paperwhite
or another app or e-reader that doesn't put out blue light.) People have monetized this already, of course, so you can get cute
little "beds" for your phone and everything. If putting a little
500-thread-count duvet on your iPhone means you'll feel comfortable leaving it in another room, then I fully endorse that
expenditure.

Day 6

Take a social media fast. No social media use for one full day.
You're probably on social media sites that I'm not cool enough
to know about, so I'll trust that you are thinking of all the ones
you use, from Snapchat to LinkedIn to YouTube to Pinterest
(and, yes, other apps like Venmo are technically social media
sites, which you might not realize). I no longer have social
apps on my phone and log in with a browser when I use social
media. Not having such constant easy access to them makes me
happier. What about you? When you're off social apps, do you
feel happier? You'll never know until you try it. Super Women

like Emma Stone and Jennifer Lawrence don't even use social media . . . and they are doing just fine.

<u>Day 7</u>
Unplug for a whole entire day. Like, no phone, no internet, #nofilter. Nada. And I don't mean keep your phone with you but put it in a pocket on vibrate or face it down as that creates the same effect of being distracted because you know it's there. So the only way to actually not be distracted is to not have it with you. You can do eeet! This is your final exam, but also the beginning of a new chapter in your digital life.

Ironically enough, there are apps out there that help you track the time you spend on your phone, and others that help with digital detox by sending you notifications when you've been sitting on one screen for too long. If you check your phone's settings and preferences, you might also have a way to manage screen time and schedule shutdown time. This idea might seem a little backward, but if you want to try these apps as part of your commitment to technology moderation, be my guest. Just keep it real with yourself and be aware of the temptation to check out other apps after a minute on these.

Regardless of how and where you accomplish it, I promise you will make it out of this detox alive. It's not as serious as some of the actual "digital detox" programs out there, which charge thousands of dollars to basically take your phone away. I tried some of them, so you don't have to. Some of them came with dieting plans and a bunch of chanting meditation things that I'm not into, and I don't think you'd be, either. So, don't have FOMO (fear of missing out)—have JOMO (joy of missing out) because you're saving your time, your money, and your mood.

So, DIY your digital detox, mindfully, remembering how being a technojunkie affects your life, from the prefrontal cortex to the corner office.

YOUR DIGITAL DIET MAINTENANCE PLAN

Now that you've made it through your seven-day detox (woohoo!), it's time to put your long-term "technology plan" in place. This is all about deciding how much, and how often, you want devices in your day-to-day life. The details are up to you. But to get you going, here are the strategies and boundaries I've come up with to find my digital balance.

Phone-Free Zones

First, I made a list of places not to use the phone, or at least to limit my phone use. Adding a spot to the list didn't mean I can never use my phone there, but it gives me the self-awareness to at least consider whether I really need to have it in my hand:

- The bathroom (because . . . really?!)
- The elevator (because I love breaking the awkwardness by actually saying "Hi!" to people)
- In a cab or ride share (because there are some pretty interesting drivers to talk to if you get your face out of whatever you are scrolling through long enough to make conversation)
- Walking in the city (because it's dangerous)
- Driving (because it's *illegal* and dangerous)

Old-School Tools

I also brought back some of the traditional tools that smartphones have replaced to help me kick the final stages of my phone habit. We often ask, "What did we do before [iPhones, Amazon, mobile banking, etc.]??" Well, the short answer is . . . pretty much the same things we do now, only slower. Faster is great, but while technology can connect you to the world, it can also disconnect you. It should improve your life, not become your life. The good news is that you probably don't need to use your phone for lots of the things you're using it for now. I'm not suggesting you dust off your DVD player and Walkman, but here are my top old-school tricks to stay on track with your "technology plan":

1. *Read a real newspaper once a week.* The news cycle is all the same stuff repeated all day long for the entire week, anyway. And for a former network news anchor, rationing my breaking-news consumption is . . . breaking news. If I can do it, you definitely can.

2. *Invest in a watch you love.* Believe it or not, a watch is actually more than a fashion statement. It also *tells time* so you don't have to wake up your phone screen to see if you're running late.

3. *Buy an actual alarm clock.* I have one at home, and on the road I use an iPod, which still has an alarm but nothing else to tempt me. I also use my iPod while running, so I can listen to music without annoying text notifications giving me the temptation to write back while I'm running (don't be that girl!).

4. *Get a planner.* They make actual planners that you can write in. I know. I have one. I don't use mine for

everything—sometimes, especially at work, you can't beat digital reminders and notifications—but it's especially nice for weekend stuff. I love writing down and being mindful of plans to look forward to.

5. *Make lists on paper.* I use two notepads every day. Why two, Lapin? Well, one has my to-do list on it and the other has my "have-done" list. Try it. If you start to feel stressed-out looking at your to-do list, then look at all the stuff you've accomplished on the "have-done" list.

6. *Invest in a sound system that isn't just your phone and some earbuds.* It doesn't need to be a record player (although bonus hipster points for using one of those), but listening to music at home, letting the sound fill your space, and taking the time to enjoy it is *so* much better than listening to it in one ear while you're ordering a sandwich. (My go-to chillout song is "Into the Mystic" by Van Morrison. It always calms me down, even though I've probably played it a thousand times. But it just doesn't sound the same hearing it while I'm asking for spicy mustard.)

7. *Buy a basic calculator.* You don't need some intricate graphing model that does calculus, just something that you can use when paying your bills or figuring out that raise you're gonna ask for—without getting distracted by your phone. Don't make a silly mistake because you're flipping back and forth between the calculator app and incoming texts.

Research has shown that a majority of people would rather go without food and other daily staples than be without their mobile devices. Was that study done in Crazytown, USA?! You know what's also old-school? Priorities. Let's bring those back, too.

A pretty good thinker named Albert Einstein once said, "I fear the day when technology will surpass our human interaction; the world will have a generation of idiots." Super Women are a lot of things but idiotic is not one of them. So, it's time to bring back some of these time-honored tools that do the job just as well as (and sometimes better than!) the phone.

KEEPING IT BASIC DOESN'T MAKE YOU A BASIC BITCH

I know: you just have to snag the latest and greatest phone. But, what if . . . you kept the phone you already have, which still works just fine? The new model obviously comes with lots of new, cool features, but more cool features means more time you'll waste test-driving them.

FYI

Some Super Women like Tyra Banks, Sarah Jessica Parker, and Rihanna have reportedly opted to buy "dumb phones" instead of smartphones, or those that *only* act as a phone.

I've interviewed a lot of amazing people who have started or run huge companies. And this might surprise you (it sure surprised me), but many of them use flip phones. I met Sir Philip Green, who runs Topshop, and he showed me his device; he's used the same model for years. In fact, he bought like twenty of them so he would never run out (like you might stock up on your favorite lipstick color in case it gets discontinued). Sir Philip is a smart dude. He could figure out an iPhone if he wanted. But he doesn't. He takes all of his calls on his OG flip phone and then moves on to the next thing without getting sucked into an email or checking up on social media.

Another person I admire for her technology awareness is Wendy Williams. I've been a regular on her show for years and recently learned that she doesn't use email. Her assistant reads or prints out the important emails for her, and that's that. Total in-box Zen. Now, we can't all have an assistant to screen our email, but we can all learn something from the way Wendy—one of the hardest-working women on TV—optimizes her time. I'd say it's worked out pretty well for her. Cue: "*How you doin'?!*"

YOUR SOBER ADVANTAGE

It's easy for me to tell you to put down your f-ing phone, but it's not so easy to actually put the f-ing thing down—and leave it there. I get it. I've relapsed—and come back from it—multiple times. Eventually it became easier, because each time I returned to the screens I realized that the digital life I was missing was nowhere near as fun as my memory made it out to be. That's when I started focusing instead on what I *gained* rather than what I missed by being offline, and so can you:

	WHAT YOU'LL MISS	**WHAT YOU'LL GAIN**
News	Yep, you'll miss out on "8 tricks to create a smoky eye," National Donut Day, and the tantalizing details of the latest celebrity trial proceedings. You'll also miss out on the quick-hit headlines and listicles, distilling important world news into a single, colorful infographic. How will you possibly go on with your day??	In-depth, substantive coverage on the most important news stories of the week, which you've read in an actual, physical newspaper and will give you way more to talk about at your next cocktail party than the best listicle out there.
Friends	You'll miss out on your bestie sharing her crazy stories, which waste an hour of your time on text but would be a four-minute conversation if you had a real one instead. And, you'll think you have way more "friends" than you actually do by obsessing over how many followers you have instead of focusing on being a leader. IRL.	Thoughtful, in-person conversations and memories that you actually remember—in your brain, not through a series of snaps. Connecting with a friend in an intimate way boosts more than just your mood; research has shown that social interactions change the circuit activity in your brain, boosting your dopamine, too.

	WHAT YOU'LL MISS	WHAT YOU'LL GAIN
Social Media	You're missing an entire photo album of the new car a friend of your mom's daughter got for her birthday and what some Kardashian girl is eating for breakfast. And you're missing out on the opportunity to obsess over which pictures you should post from events you weren't present at, taking the perfect picture that you still edit fifty times with another fifty filters. Oh, and you're definitely missing trolling your ex-boyfriend's feeds for which of your mutual friends are following his new girlfriend.	Awareness of everything happening around you, from the smell of fresh-cut grass to the way the wind ruffles your dress to how delicious your coconut ice cream tastes. You'll also gain perspective: that your life is the one worth living, not the many other lives you happen to follow on social media.
Romantic Relationships	You are definitely missing out on obsessing over text messages from a new guy you're into, or an old flame you wish would come back around. You're also missing out on being at a party, event, or bar full of hot bachelors and not paying any attention to them because you are swiping through your phone.	The opportunity to meet someone great, in person, by striking up conversation—in person. And you might even gain a partner.

	WHAT YOU'LL MISS	**WHAT YOU'LL GAIN**
Work	You'll miss writing quick, impulsive emails instead of being thoughtful and professional about your approach. You'll also miss out on having actual phone calls and meetings with the people you work with because you are using one-sentence or even one-word emails as a proxy for conversation.	Greater focus at work, which will improve your overall performance. "But, people expect me to respond within a few minutes, Lapin!" Oh, really? Why do they expect that? Because you've always responded within a few minutes before. You train people to adapt to your email habits just by doing them. Stepping away from the email treadmill you are running on in order to really think a situation through will give you the biggest edge yet.

When it comes right down to it, you're just not missing out on that much valuable stuff by sticking to a reasonable relationship with your phone. The most important thing you can do to wean off the smartphone security blanket is focus on rebooting and nurturing a rich offline life. If you relapse as you try to implement a sustainable "technology plan," try an abridged detox or do a little quick rehab by:

1. Setting up "do not disturb" functionality that lets you hear from, say, your son but no one else

2. Creating "digital free zones" at work and home where Wi-Fi is literally blocked in certain rooms
3. Separating your personal and business accounts or numbers

SUPER WOMAN TIP

Lead the (Un)Charge

Errors at work increase by 28 percent after getting a phone call and 23 percent after getting a text, according to a study from Florida State University. That means that if you limit calls and texts while at work, then you already have a 28 percent and 23 percent advantage, respectively, over colleagues who don't. One trick for holding yourself accountable is just not bringing a charger with you to the office. (Sure, you can borrow one, but . . . don't.) The battery doesn't die on your phone while it's just sitting there minding its own business. The more you use it, the more your battery dies. So, live a little and it will live, too.

Now, lest you think I'm a downer on all things smartphone, let me just say: It's all about being mindful of your usage (we have a whole step on that coming up next). Our phones can be some of the best tools out there, as we discussed earlier, but only if we keep them solidly in that "tools" category of our lives and not make them an obsession. It's pretty incredible that you can Skype with a relative halfway around the world. Getting a Lyft when it's raining is awesome (for you and your hair). Managing your personal finances, checking in with your monthly budget, and making credit card payments is way more laborious (not to mention, unfriendly to trees) without that banking app on your phone. The list could go on for the rest of this book. My point is that using your phone for specific tasks and then being done with it gives you an A in efficiency—and Super Women are nothing if not efficient AF.

CHECK IN AND CHECK OUT

So did you manage it? The "one check" challenge for the entirety of this chapter? If so, are you up for another?

If you don't check your phone at all until you finish this book, email me at nicole@becomingsuperwomanbook.com. As a reward, I will send a friend of your choice an e-book so that she, too, can become a Super Woman.

Oh, and if you don't have her email address, do me a favor—just pick up the phone and call her to ask for it. Catch up, tell her about the book (and how much you love it, obviously), and then tell her about this little challenge. You might also find out something about her life . . . before she posts about it on social media.

BOTTOM LINE

Conventional Wisdom: Smartphones are how we stay connected in today's world.

Seventy percent of people with smartphones keep them "within eye distance" at work. What else do you keep within eye distance at all times at work? Maybe a picture of your family or your dog? One of these items is worthwhile, and one isn't. Studies have shown that we gain more brain power and achieve more success from making actual connections with our colleagues, friends, and family than virtual ones.

Conventional Wisdom: I don't need to do a full digital detox, as long as I keep the idea of using my phone less in mind.

Mmmkay . . . keep that "in mind." That's like saying you're going to get in shape by "keeping it in mind" to go to the gym. Solid plans keep you accountable and aware of your behaviors. You may get to a point where putting your phone away is totally normal for you. But if that day is not today (and let's be honest, for most of us it's not) then you should really consider the full digital detox shebang.

Conventional Wisdom: Advantages at work come from . . . hard work. So, if I do all my work, who cares if I take a break to look at my phone?

Well, *you* should care, that's who. How often does that five-minute break actually stop at five minutes? Doing good work is a *baseline*. It's not something unique to you, it's expected (as an employer, I know that). What sets you apart and gets you ahead are the advantages others *don't* have. The advantage of working with both hands (like, without your smartphone in one of them) is a smart place to start.

STEP

8

BE MINDFUL—NOT MIND FULL

Make Mindfulness Your New Superpower

Quick: What is the title of this step? You just read it. Do you need to go back and read it again? Were you thinking about what you were going to have for dinner while you were "reading" it? Or checking your phone, again (which we *just* went over in the last step)? Or, were you mindfully reading the title as "Be Mindful—Not Mind Full"?

Mindfulness is a buzzy concept these days, but it's really just the practice of being aware. That's all. It's being aware of what you are doing when you are doing it.

Earlier in the book you outlined how you plan to spend your time. It's one of the toughest decisions you'll make over and over again. You could have been one hundred different places, doing one hundred different things right now. But once you've decided what that one place and one thing will be, this step comes in—to teach you how to fully *be* wherever you are and fully *do* whatever you're doing.

PRESENT YOURSELF

Mindfulness is not a clinical, cold technique that involves using your "mind" unemotionally, like a calculator. In some Asian languages, the words "mind" and "heart" are actually the same word. So think of "mindfulness" as nearly interchangeable with "heartfulness." It's intended to help you be and feel more aware—of how you treat yourself, how you act toward others, and of your environment—so you make informed choices as to how you spend your time; choices that are in accordance with your values.

As you prepare to learn how to fill your mind with mindfulness, it helps to take a baseline of where you're at. So, how mindful are you now?

MINDFULNESS PULSE CHECK:

1. Does your mind tend to wander during conversations that last more than ten seconds?

2. Do you spend conversations thinking about what you are going to say next instead of listening to what's being said now?

3. Do you check your phone during conversations, use it during meetings, and keep it on the table during meals? (Ahem. Hopefully not—after the last step!)

4. Do you get from one place to another and realize you have no memory of the walk or drive you just took?

5. Do you have trouble taking one task to completion before wandering off to start something new?

6. Do you frequently make impulsive decisions or blurt out whatever comes to mind?

7. Do you get so overwhelmed by your jumble of thoughts or feelings that you feel paralyzed and unable to make decisions or articulate opinions?

This is not SAT-style scoring. The more you answered "yes" above, the more of a problem you have staying present. But that's okay. Mindfulness is a skill—like the other steps in the book or riding a bike or applying liquid eyeliner. You can and will get better at it.

BE LIKE BEY

I've said this before, but I'll remind you again because I remind myself *all* the time: You have the same number of hours in the day as Beyoncé. Sure, she has an army of people who help her get ready and get around, but at the end of the day, she has twenty-four hours to make the most of each day just like we do (and as I told you in Step 3, has the same struggle with burnout). In previous steps, you figured out how to make the most of those hours. Now let me tell you about another superpower of Queen B's, one I've personally witnessed: Queen B knows how to just *be*.

How many fans do you think Beyoncé has? I'm not sure numbers even go that high. But have you ever asked one of those fans lucky enough to have met her how the Queen made them feel? Well, I will be the ultimate fangirl right now and tell you that when I met Beyoncé, she looked me in the eye and said, genuinely, "Nice to meet you." And for the few moments we were talking, she wasn't looking at her phone or glancing around the room, she was totally focused on the fan right in front of her: me. Which, in turn, made me even more of a fan (which I didn't think was possible). And from what I hear, my experience is pretty much standard—she gives everyone the royal treatment. Keep that in mind as you build your own castle . . . mindfully, of course.

Remember Everyone's Name

Making a note of someone's name when you first meet them is more about mindfulness than having an airtight memory. So the next time someone introduces themselves to you at a dinner party, *listen*. Then repeat it back to them. Then repeat it back to yourself. Remembering someone's name shows them you care and forges a connection with them right from the get-go; forgetting it shows the opposite. Try this:

New Friend: "Hi, Super Woman, my name is Nicole."

You: Repeat the name "Nicole" one or two times in your head and say, "Nice to meet you, Nicole."

New Friend: "It's great to meet you, too . . . yada yada yada."

You: Before the conversation heats up, think of a Nicole you already know or a household name like Nicole Kidman or Nicole Richie and associate your new friend with them. Memory experts say that the more we can familiarize ourselves with a new person within a few minutes of meeting them, the more likely we are to form a memorable bond with them. You can also find a distinguishing feature of theirs to call their name to mind, like Nicole's moles (just maybe . . . don't say that one out loud). Then turn back to listen closely to the conversation at hand—the real one, not the one you were just having in your head.

New Friend: "Yada, yada, yada . . . love to follow up on email."

You: "Absolutely, Nicole." On your way home, review the people you met at the party—including Nicole—*by name*, as well as what you talked about, and then follow up as promised to reinforce the new relationship, dropping in a few memorable tidbits from your conversation to show her that you valued her time, and also to further reinforce your memory of the exchange.

If remembering names is a challenge for you, the problem probably isn't retention. It's mindfulness. In fact, being present is the number-one tip all memory experts give when helping people remember names. Your own name is said to be the most powerful sound you can hear. Imagine being in a crowded concert hall with sensory overload and someone calls out your name. What will stand out the most? The band? The crowd? Nope—your name. So what's in a name, Juliet? Actually, a lot.

Attention is time, and time is money. We've all wished there were more hours in the day. Paying attention to how you spend your time and making the people you spend it with feel priceless is the closest you'll get to finding them.

Arianna Huffington, founder of the *Huffington Post* and CEO of Thrive Global, talks a lot about "sleeping your way to the top." While I'm all about taking care of yourself and incorporating ample sleep into the schedule you established back in Step 6, the truth is that it takes a lot of waking hours to get ahead, especially early on in your career. You can't take over the world when you're fast asleep. But what if you set out making your waking hours more mindful instead? By making every single hour count, you may just find that those long days feel shorter—and become more productive.

MIND YOUR *P*s

Being present is at the core of being mindful. Mindfulness changes the way you see, hear, touch, smell, and taste. It will change the way you interact with people. It will change your mood and productivity. It's the most readily available game changer there is—and one that most people forget about the moment they hop out of bed and, especially, when they step into work mode.

Mindfulness techniques help us to slow down and act more intentionally in the face of constant distraction. There are stacks on stacks on stacks of books dedicated to the art of staying present and mindful in various areas of your life. Mindful eating is a big category, for example; simply paying attention to your food and how you feel while you eat—instead of watching TV or scrolling through your phone—will make a difference in your eating habits faster than anything else. But we rarely talk about "mindfulness at work."

The mindfulness principles I've learned have been most helpful for me in my career. Becoming more mindful in *every* area of my life has yielded some of my greatest business ideas, insights, and wins. And I'm going to give you a simple framework you can use to become a mindfulness master yourself. After all, we're called human *beings*, not human *doings*. Learn to *be*, first and foremost, and the doing will come.

You know I love me some alliteration every chance I get. So, *ta-da*! I hereby present the three *P*s of Mindfulness:

*P*ause. Take a beat. Take a breath.

*P*rocess. What are you feeling? What is actually happening—not in your imagination but in reality?

*P*ounce. Now that you know what is happening, determine the best thing to do in response. Then do it.

Whether it's planning proactively or problem-solving (a few more *P*s for the alliteration win!), *pausing* to *process* a situation helps you *pounce* more thoughtfully—and ultimately more successfully. But while the cutesy alliteration might make this seem easy peasy, it's not. The words are simple; the implementation takes serious practice.

A CAUSE TO *PAUSE*

Pausing is a skill. It's one of the most important ones in charting the direction of your career. That's because that direction is ultimately made up of all your individual decisions. Every day we make some thousands of them. Every big decision we make is made up of thousands of other baby decisions. And before making those decisions, whether with your mind or your gut, you have to pause.

Often, we don't even realize we are making a decision, much less that we are pausing before it. Research shows that pausing for fifty to one hundred milliseconds helps the brain focus on the information relevant for the decision while blocking out distractions. You can pause for a millisecond, or you can pause for a week. Sometimes the decision (soup or salad?)

doesn't matter, so neither does the pause. But the more important the decision, the more important that pause becomes.

I am queen of the knee-jerk reaction. Saying whatever comes to mind works fine with people who already know and love my quirky self, but it's gotten me into trouble with work folks. And it's something I've really had to work on.

For a long time, I was uncomfortable whenever there was a pause in a conversation. Another verbal jab or sparring opener would fly out of my mouth to fill the space. Being a news anchor for so long, I dreaded any dead air. But these pauses encourage people to open up and make room for creative ideas and thoughtful responses. When I stopped trying to medal in verbal gymnastics, I realized that sometimes, silence really is golden.

Now, it's one thing to be mindful during calm, friendly conversations. It's another thing when you're feeling frustration or anger toward someone. It's easy to say you will pause the next time you find yourself ready to go on the offensive or about to have a panic attack. But once you're faced with it, pausing can feel impossible. So, don't face the pause on your own. Enter: your mindfulness guardian angel.

Sometimes, when I'm pausing, I ask myself: *What Would Ellen Do?* No, not Ellen DeGeneres, although she is awesome. My bestie, Ellen, is the most positive person I know. She has the purest values, morals, and intentions. So, whenever I start feeling a devilish impulse, I think about what my real-life guardian angel Ellen would do, and then I do that instead. For example, if I'm considering firing off a nasty email in response to a message that seems unfair, I'll pause instead, think about what Ellen would do, and then pick up the phone to call the person to talk through the miscommunication. Pausing to think of Ellen reminds me to be more mindful of my actions and how they will help or hurt the situation. So, who is your Ellen?

> **FYI**
>
> The HALT System recognizes that when you're Hungry, Angry, Lonely, or Tired, you're most likely to make poor decisions. Don't let these negative stressors trigger the wrong choice. If you're HALT, then halt decision-making until you're not.

Pausing during tense times gets a lot easier once you make it a habit. Try putting up a reminder note listing the 3 Ps, somewhere you're likely to see it before you shoot off an email you'll regret, like on your computer screen. Then keep your emotions from taking over by noticing what's going on physically—your body, your breath. Try the "BFF method" where you simply breathe and feel your feet. Unclench your hands and jaw. Relax your face muscles, palms, and tummy. Get out of your head. Tap into your senses with the "5, 4, 3, 2, 1" method: notice five things you see, four things you can touch, three things you can hear, two things you can smell, and one thing you can taste. Get up. Walk around. I often take a little ride up and down in the elevator for a breather. The motion and the people watching takes the edge off and gives me the pause I need to move on to the next step: processing what's happening and deciding what I should do about it.

Ice, Ice Baby

SUPER WOMAN TIP

There's a reason you see professional athletes chilling in huge tubs of ice on the sidelines at halftime; it's not just to bring down swelling from the hits taken on the field. Ice has a real physiological benefit. It brings your heart rate back to normal quickly and redirects your blood where it's needed the most: to your heart and internal organs. Holding an ice cube is often recommended by therapists as a grounding exercise—the physical sensation of shocking cold is so intense that it demands your attention and forces you into the present (and out of your own head). You can cool yourself down with an ice cube, or by pressing a cold washcloth or chilled drink from the vending machine against your skin. If you're at home, take a cold shower or fill a large bowl with icy water and submerge your face for a few moments. I'm serious: when you're heated, ice does wonders for your body and your mind.

TRUST THE *PROCESS*

Let's say a deal you've been working on for months just imploded. And you're on the verge of doing so yourself. You're spinning, overwhelmed. You find it in you to *pause* before rattling off a nasty email or bursting into tears at your desk. But, you still feel out of control—so what do you do now?

Process. Name the emotions.

It might not seem like a big deal to explicitly say "I am angry," but it is. When you are breathless and flustered, the events feel too chaotic to explain and the emotions feel too heightened to describe. Forcing yourself to articulate *exactly* what you are feeling makes it more manageable to process.

Naming is a major part of mindfulness. Neurological studies have shown that when you're experiencing an emotion, describing it in a few words actually reduces that emotion. When you give a name to the awfulness that's taking you over, you give yourself some much-needed distance from it.

And when it comes to naming emotions, you actually don't have many options. As I learned throughout the many behavioral seminars I've taken, there are really *just* five core emotions to choose from: anger, disgust, fear, happiness, sadness. These five are brought to life in *Inside Out*, one of the greatest Disney movies since *The Little Mermaid*. Super Woman Mindy Kaling, who played the voice of Disgust in the movie, said she broke down in tears when she first read the script. She said, "I think it's really beautiful that [Disney] is making a story that tells kids it's difficult to grow up and that it's okay to be sad about it."

Of course, we are growing up at every age (because growing old is mandatory but growing up is optional), and it can always be tricky to name your emotions, especially when you're in crisis mode. You can also be feeling more than one of the five at a time. But there's no quota, so name all of them. And while this looks like a chart you'd see at the doctor's office, I've found it helpful when emotions feel jumbled and difficult for me to articulate.

ANGER

Feelings to describe anger: Infuriated, insecure, jealous, threatened, skeptical, frustrated, distant, hurt, critical, violated

Physical changes and expressions of anger: Muscles tightening; hands clenching; feeling your face flush or get hot; feeling like you're going to explode; wanting to hit someone, bang the wall, or throw something

Effects of anger: Narrowing attention, attending only to the situation that's making you angry; ruminating about the situation making you angry or about situations in the past; imagining future situations that will make you angry

DISGUST

Feelings to describe disgust: Disapproval, loathing, disappointed, hesitant, judgmental, avoidance, aversion, revulsion

Physical changes and expressions of disgust: Decreased heart rate; wrinkling your nose and/or sticking out your tongue; nausea; body chills; wanting to turn or run away

Effects of disgust: Difficulty making rational decisions; focusing purely on removing yourself from the situation or thing making you disgusted; dehumanizing the object of your disgust

FEAR

Feelings to describe fear: Anxious, insecure, submissive, rejected, humiliated, scared, overwhelmed, worried, inadequate, worthless

Physical changes and expressions of fear: Quickened heart rate; shortness of breath; heightened awareness; jitters; sweaty palms and feet; headaches; stomachaches; nausea

Effects of fear: Inability to make important decisions; irrational or unethical thinking; reacting impulsively

HAPPINESS

Feelings to describe happiness: Optimistic, powerful, peaceful, accepted, proud, interested, joyful, confident, loving, playful

Physical changes and expressions of happiness: Smiling or laughing; quickened heart rate; urge to run or jump; warmth in the face and extremities; sensation of lightness

Effects of happiness: Focusing on the moment at hand; appreciation for what you have; appreciation for yourself and those in your life; confidence in your abilities

SADNESS

Feelings to describe sadness: Guilty, abandoned, despair, lonely, bored, ignored, inferior, apathetic, empty, ashamed

Physical changes and expressions of sadness: Feeling tired, run-down, or low energy; feeling lethargic/wanting to stay in bed all day; feeling empty; difficulty swallowing; crying; breathlessness or dizziness

Effects of sadness: Blaming or criticizing yourself; sleeping and eating too much or too little; yearning for something else

Naming what you're really feeling the most can change your response to an event. Let's say a friend forgot your birthday. At first you might feel irritated (angry) and want to lash out. But, upon further emotion naming, you might also discover that you are feeling abandoned (sad) and, instead, call her up for a heart-to-heart conversation about it. Recognizing emotions helps you respond appropriately in a way you're proud (happy) of.

I know that emotions feel like they will last forever (take it from the girl who has been told her entire life that she "holds on to things too long" or "can't shake it"). But, while emotions are a complex biochemical process in the body, not a subjective feeling, they are programmed to only last thirty to forty seconds if played out. Think about how fast a baby can go from giggly to hysterically crying. We are prewired to shift emotional states very quickly. But you can't just make an emotion "go away." Trying to do that only makes it last longer and makes you focus on it more. The best way to get back to a "baby's mind" (or "beginner's mind" as mindfulness gurus call it) as an adult is to name the emotion to tame it. The more you resist acknowledging it, the more it persists.

There's an inner tape (or MP3) for all of us that's cued every time we are triggered by emotions. Most of the tracks are negative, which makes sense if you remember the "negativity bias" I brought up in Step 1 and notice that only one of the five named emotions is positive. My biggest hit is, "How did I fuck that up? I fucked up my life." Mindfulness helps us hear the track even if it's old vinyl from the past, but balance helps us change it. To play a different tune, you must have other tunes to play. Throughout the rest of the book, we'll talk more about how you can create more positivity in your life and thereby more positive jams to dance to. There will always be shitty songs. If you want to take them off repeat, you need to have a new beat to bring in. But, first, you have to record it.

Your body is designed to help you if you let it. The heart secretes something called atrial natriuretic peptide (ANP). It is the primary way to combat cortisol (a distress hormone) in the body. I know it's the most annoying thing to hear when you're upset, but, actually, the best way to initiate ANP is to smile. Forced smiles count, too, as they often turn into real ones. So dig deep for a smile, a giggle, or a whistle—your body can actually trick your mind into lifting your mood.

FYI

"Just leave the emotion out of it" is common business advice, especially for women, but I couldn't disagree more. When someone asks me, "How do you feel about being a woman in business?" I often say, "a lot." Now, part of that is just my usual smart assery, but I do strongly believe that you don't need to be an ice queen to be a Super Woman. One of the most *helpful,* not hurtful, things about being a woman in business is our ability to use our "female" traits like empathy, patience, and vulnerability. These traits that are inherently emotional can be our greatest superpowers if we view them that way. They give us a naturally higher EQ, half of the Emotional Wellness equation (remember, *emotional intelligence + mental wellness = Emotional Wellness*).

Think It Through

In addition to naming emotions, part of processing is labeling the thoughts you have, especially the recurring ones. As with emotions, labeling your thoughts helps you get some perspective on them when they feel all-consuming. I imagine those thoughts as logs floating along a river. I see each one and give it a shout-out: "Hey, what's up 'obsessing over the ex'?" or "Oh, hello again 'self doubt'!" I name my thoughts and let them keep rolling down the river, even if there is a whole forest of them.

Sometimes you have to wait and watch for a while, but eventually you'll see a different kind of log come along. "Hey, it's 'reveling in my amazing accomplishment' and 'grateful for my kick-ass friends!'" Take note of each and every thought as it comes down the line, and you'll begin to see how they all come together to build the beautiful, strong structure that is you—'obsessing over the ex' included. Mindfulness hinges on the acceptance of yourself for who you are and where you are at that moment. Whatever you are feeling or thinking, observe it honestly and don't hate on yourself.

CONFESSIONS
OF A SUPER WOMAN

Don't Talk About My Friend Like That

"My television career is over," I huffed as I plopped into William's chair for an "air cut" (what I call my trims).

"I doubt that," William said calmly, like the amateur shrink all good hairdressers are.

Over more than a decade, William has become more than just my hair stylist, colorist, and extension coiffeur extraordinaire. In fifteen years, I've lived in ten cities: Los Angeles, Chicago, Philadelphia, Palm Springs, Sioux Falls, Lexington, San Francisco, Paris, Atlanta, and New York. Every time I move, I find new people, but I never cheat on my longtime golden highlight master, William. If I have roots that are five inches long, then I will have roots that are five inches long until I can see William again. (Ombre is in anyway, right?)

"No, it is. I'm so stupid, I can't believe I butchered that equation for compounding interest on-air. How could I have done that? It's not the producer's fault; it was my responsibility to check before going on. I'm such an idiot. They are never going to have me on again and my credibility is shot. People who saw the segment are already writing bad reviews for my book . . . Did you know you can review something on Amazon that you didn't even buy?! That's so fucked up. My book sales are going to tank and I'm done."

"I watched the segment—your hair looked great, at least," William said with a laugh, trying to lighten the mood.

"It's not funny, William. I'll be marching my golden locks down to the unemployment line. I'm so mad at myself," I said, nervously picking at my nails and scrolling through my phone. "I suck."

"Okay, stop talking about my friend like that!" William snapped at me suddenly, clicking the scissors in the air to get me to look at him in the mirror instead of incessantly checking for backlash online.

"Wait, who? What?" I said, confused and on the verge of tears. "Which friend?"

"*You!* My friend is brilliant, passionate, and kind. She doesn't suck. She is *not* an idiot. And I'm not going to let you talk about my friend like that."

As I looked him in the eye, I started to understand.

"Would you just stand by and let someone say *I* sucked?!" William asked, pointing the scissors at me in the mirror.

"No."

"Exactly. And I'm not going to stand around and let someone say *you* suck, even if it's you."

I paused. William had all the power—after all, he was holding scissors next to my head.

"Okay, just don't get mad at the hair," I said, half-smiling.

"Your career isn't over," he said, returning to my air cut. "You'll have hundreds of other appearances. You made a mistake. You're doing way too much and there's no way all of it can be one hundred percent. You're brilliant, but you're also human. You'll say you're sorry and clarify. You'll have hundreds of good reviews and those few haters aren't going to matter. Okay?"

I cut short my self-hating diatribe. It seemed that if I didn't have anything nice to say about myself, I shouldn't say anything at all. So I didn't.

I was quiet for the rest of my time in the chair that night, maybe the most silence William had ever gotten from me before. And the most he has gotten

> since, because by the next time I saw him, I had made
> up with his "friend."

I have a long track record of catastrophizing work problems, making them feel more dire than they actually are. (BTW, the word "catastrophizing" comes from "catastrophe," which means "a momentous tragic event ranging from extreme misfortune to utter overthrow or ruin." When was the last time you were truly on the verge of *utter overthrow or ruin*? Right. Me neither.) If something didn't go my way or I made a mistake, I would leap to the conclusion that I'd become broke and homeless. Seriously. Now, that wasn't realistic or rational, but that's what the voice inside my head told me.

For example, let's say I lost a TV development deal I'd been working on for six months.

Here's how my supercritical inner voice would describe what happened: *I failed. I disappointed myself and my team. I lost a TV development deal I'd been working on for six months. This deal was going to make or break the company. This will give us a bad reputation of not closing deals, and others won't want to work with us. I will have to let go of awesome people who have families to support, and I won't be able to support myself. I won't be able to afford rent, and because I don't have parents to bail me out when I'm in trouble, I will end up homeless.*

If I cut out all the editorializing from that description, the truth remained just the third sentence: *I lost a TV development deal I'd been working on for six months.*

Do you do this kind of catastrophizing? Not sure? Once you have processed your feelings and thoughts, you need to process the situation. And just like with them, this means describing it accurately. Write out the story of something bad that happened to you recently. Go back and cross out all the self-judgment, which is basically like breaking your own heart, so let's not do that. Then take out the hypothetical worst-case scenarios you are inserting into that story. What's left? Those are the facts.

A THREE-STEP PROCESS TO PROCESS ANY SITUATION

First: *Fact find.* Don't sensationalize what happened. For example, let's say your coworker got a promotion. That's what you write down. You don't write down anything about how they are the worst and your boss hates you and you got hosed. Just the facts, ma'am. If you're looking to figure out past situations, keep in mind that memories come with our own confirmation bias, which causes our brain to store information that's consistent with our own beliefs and values. We are our own mini echo chamber, which makes it even more important to tune in to the facts.

Second: *Check the facts.* Check those facts against the list of what's awesome in your life that we put together back in Step 2. Did the event jeopardize anything on there? Most likely it didn't. Then ask yourself: "Does my emotional response fit the facts?" Your feelings—anger, disgust, sadness, etc.—are valid, but if you are having a total meltdown over a coworker getting a promotion, the *magnitude* of your response is probably out of proportion to what actually happened. Mindfulness helps us figure out the difference between the underlying stress and the distress we create on top of it.

Third: Imagine. I know, I know, your point of view is super important and it's special because it's yours. But even if it's the last thing you want to do, try to look at the situation from other perspectives. Are there any upsides? Are your emotions the result of assumptions that aren't based in reality? For instance, if you responded to your coworker's promotion with the thought "my boss hates me," consider whether you can think of other explanations for her decision. Often we think that we "know" what someone else is thinking. But unless you're a psychic, you don't. You only know what *you* are thinking. If you want to know what someone else is thinking, *ask them*. Don't give a thousand-dollar response to a nickel event by imagining conflict or catastrophes that may not even exist.

Check In with Yourself

SUPER WOMAN TIP

When you feel like the world is ending, check in with yourself about it, and ask yourself questions to figure out if it really, truly is. Seriously.

Say you get into this funk right before you need to go to sleep. Ask yourself: *What is happening right now?*

Then answer: *Well, I am lying in bed. There is a sheet below me and a fluffy comforter on top of me. I am wiggling my toes and cracking my ankles.*

Does that sound like the world is ending? Are you about to get attacked by a bear or smashed by a boulder??

No, there is no bear. There is no boulder. I guess the world is not technically ending right now.

Okay, good. Stop cracking your ankles and go to sleep.

Our imaginations have the power to create and destroy. Yours can paint a picture of you running the world, or of being crushed by the weight of it. Mindfulness helps us remember that things are often scarier in our imagination than reality.

When your brain thinks you're in danger, it automatically goes into fight-or-flight mode as a survival skill. Essentially, if your body thinks there's a threat or you're under attack or under acute stress, it prepares to fight or flee the perceived danger. This is actually a quite useful response if something legitimately life-threatening is going on. But just because it happens automatically, it doesn't mean it's accurate or appropriate. For example, you could have the same fight-or-flight response (some include freeze as a third option) if you're being held captive or if you're scared to speak in front of a crowd. Mindfulness helps you determine which is life-threatening and which is not so that *you* can choose how best to react instead of being a slave to your fight-or-flight response.

GET READY TO *P*OUNCE

Decision fatigue is a real thing, what with those 35,000 we have to make each and every day. Iced or Hot? Tall or grande? Two pumps or three? One shot or two? Coconut milk or almond? For here or to go? Credit or debit? And that's just coffee.

My ex-boyfriend used to ask me if I wanted to watch an actual movie during our usual movie nights together. That's because I would watch *every single preview* on Apple TV, paralyzed by indecision, and end up not picking anything, finally leaving it up to him, hours in, rather than face the prospect of choosing the "wrong" movie. What's the worst that could have happened? I'd choose a movie, hate it, and then watch it to the end? Stop it halfway through if it was *really* bad? We all want to make the right decision, but the worst decision is always not deciding at all and watching previews all night.

Ordering coffee and picking movies are relatively low-stakes choices, but this also holds true with the higher-stakes decisions that life throws our way. You don't need all of the information, just *enough* to make a decision and move on. Indecision can be your own prison. As Super Woman Anna Wintour says, "Even if I'm completely unsure, I'll pretend I know exactly what I'm talking about and make a decision." If the Queen of *Vogue* and the Met Gala can fake it 'til she makes it with decision-making, then, sister, you can, too.

So, after you've paused and processed, it's time to decide how you are going to pounce. To do this, you need to know three things:

1. What exactly you are deciding?
2. What are your options?
3. What do you want the ultimate outcome to be?

Here's a hypothetical: *You just had your annual review and you didn't get the promotion you were expecting.*

No judgment here on your emotions, but your pounce shouldn't be driven by them. If you let emotions drive you, you might leave the job without a plan, telling your boss off on your way out. Maybe you'll still do that, but that's not a trivial "tall or grande" decision. Mindfulness techniques can help you see the big picture.

So, during your *pause* and *process* time, you manage to avoid storming out of the office in order to identify what you are feeling and find the facts of the situation. Now it's time to *pounce*.

1. *You are deciding*: Should I stay at this job?
2. *Your options are*: stay and try to get a promotion next

year; stay and plot an exit; leave with no plan; leave
with a plan.

3. *You want the ultimate outcome to be*: earn six figures.

As you look at your pouncing options, it's natural to want
to make a Pros/Cons list for each. The instinct is a good one,
but I think it's a bad idea to make a list that assigns the same
weight to each point. Why would "Sticks it to my boss" as a
Pro carry the same weight as "Can no longer feed my family"
as a Con?!

This is why you should upgrade to the Super Pros/Cons list,
which I created to help you make super tough decisions. Instead
of just listing Pros and Cons in opposing columns and then
counting them up against each other, this version is weighted
to help you make a, well, weighty decision. Think about it: the
considerations that go into making a big decision are not all
equal. Some are deal breakers, while others are merely inconve-
nient. So assigning those considerations equal weight can lead
to skewed results "for" or "against." For the Pro category, you
assign up to +5 points according to importance. For the Con
category, you assign down to −5 points depending on how serious that concern is.

Let's make a Super Pros/Cons list for the option to "Stay
and plot an exit."

Super Pros:

1. Keeps my income steady +5
2. Gives me more time to think about my next move +3
3. Doesn't violate my contract +4

Super Cons:

1. I will still have to deal with the shithead who didn't give me a promotion. −3
2. I won't do my best work because I will be distracted thinking about my next move. −5
3. I will have the same workspace that I've had for the last three years. −1

The Super Pros add up to +12.
The Super Cons add up to −9.
This Super Pros/Cons list is +3 in favor of the Pros—so the "stay and plot an exit" stays on the list.

Not only does this give you a "yes" or "no" for each option, it also helps you see how overwhelming that "yes" or "no" is. And at the end, because you don't give "keeps my income steady" and "I will have the same workspace that I've had for the last three years" the same heft, you will have an overall picture that is more representative of the weight of your deciding factors.

Once you have evaluated all of your options, you might have a couple finalists. Sometimes the best way to choose a winner is to flip your desired "ultimate outcome" and do a "reverse brainstorm." Maybe you've hit a wall trying to think of the best way to reach your goal. So, instead, think of ways *not* to reach your goal.

This is a reverse brainstorm for how to "not earn six figures":

1. Have no job
2. Get really sick
3. Have to take care of someone and be unable to work

If your true objective is to "earn six figures," then you won't get there if you have no job, so, at least for now, you have to *pounce* on a choice that includes having a job, unless you change what you want the ultimate outcome to be. So, in this case, that would likely leave you with "stay and plot an exit" and "leave with a plan" as the best options. Notice that these two options are not mutually exclusive; from this exercise, it now becomes clear that you could stay at your current job while locking down a really solid plan for the next one, instead of up and quitting with only a half-baked plan in the works. Gradually adjust your efforts at work to, say, 80 percent, so that you have more time and bandwidth outside of work to research higher-paying opportunities, apply to jobs, and go on interviews. Then, once the right opportunity comes through, you'll be ready to *pounce*!

When I look back at my own story, it's full of moments that I'm not particularly proud of. Have I failed to pause in the past? For sure. Have I pounced too recklessly? Absolutely. I remind myself that if I had known then what I know now, the outcome would likely have been different. But, I also try and remember that because I do indeed know more now, I should have better outcomes from now on.

A Super Woman tries everything in her power to live a life she's proud of. If you find that you're not living that way, you can always start all over again, just like we talked about in Step 2. But once you *are* living your super life, make sure you're really present for every minute of it—after all, you only get one.

BOTTOM LINE

Conventional Wisdom: Emotions don't belong in the workplace.

There's nowhere to check your emotions at the door, so you've gotta bring those babies in with you. Mindfulness helps you keep them in check and, in fact, use them to work toward your goals and get ahead.

Conventional Wisdom: I can't force myself to be happy.

You sure can. You might think that smiling, whistling, humming, and dancing are things you do because you're happy. But it also works the other way around. Science shows that forcing yourself to smile, whistle, hum, or dance during stressful times can create a self-fulfilling happiness prophecy. You can also touch yourself (not like *that*). Try patting yourself on the back, literally, or giving yourself a hug or holding your own hand. This has a similar effect on your mood as you'd get from someone else patting you on your back, giving you a hug, or holding your hand.

Conventional Wisdom: Making a Pros/Cons list helps me make decisions.

When faced with a decision that is weighing on you, give it the weight it deserves with a Super Pros/Cons list. This gives you the most accurate picture of what your decision should be.

Conventional Wisdom: I need to respond and make decisions right away.

Two things in life you'll never regret: 1) a good workout and 2) waiting a little while before sending an email or making an important decision.

STEP
9

MASTER THE MIND GAME

Get Down with Meditation and Mindset

"**Y**ou want me to *what*?!" If you're getting ready to flip past this chapter, saying "Lapin, I signed up for business advice, not Burning Man," just . . . hold on a second.

I've interviewed Super Women in every arena: business, fashion, politics, you name it. And while they each stand out in their own way, one quality holds true across the spectrum: they are cool (as in coolheaded). So, what's their secret? They all have serious control of their minds.

Movers and shakers in every industry have credited meditation as contributing to their biggest breakthroughs by allowing their thoughts to "breathe." After all, you can't force a genius idea. The more you try for an "aha," the more "ha ha" you'll get back from your brain. So, the way they invite genius in is by manifesting it.

In the last step, we talked about being more mindful. Now we are going to bring the mind game to another level by mastering meditation and mindset. In this step, you are going to take serious control of your mind, so that your mind doesn't take control of you.

CLEAR YOUR MIND

Meditation is not all hippie-dippie yogi stuff. In fact, there is so much science backing up its positive effects that doctors prescribe it regularly. And because they know that taking care of your mind is also good business, top companies (like Google, Facebook, Amazon) pay to bring in experts to school their execs on meditation basics and promote it heavily to their employees.

You might be saying, "I have too many thoughts, it won't work" or "That sounds cool, but I don't have the time." Well, we can *all* feel plagued with thoughts (we have sixty to eighty thousand every day) and crippled with obligations. It's even *more* reason to take your AM/PM "meds" (as in meditation) just like countless Super Women, including Ellen DeGeneres, do. Here's how Ellen describes meditation: "Kind of like when you have to shut your computer down, just sometimes when it goes crazy, you just shut it down and when you turn it on, it's okay again."

In addition to feeling recharged, meditation can provide the necessary perspective and calm to lead like a warrior . . . Padmasree Warrior, that is. She was the chief technology officer of Cisco (who also has the best name ever) and is ranked as one of the one hundred most powerful women in the world. Warrior managed more than twenty thousand employees at the IT and networking giant, and she keeps her stress level in check with a twenty-minute meditation every evening, saying "it makes me so much calmer when I'm responding to emails later."

FIVE REASONS TO MEDITATE YOUR WAY TO THE TOP

1. *Your brain.* Meditation has been shown to improve cognitive function and lessen the effects of age on your brain, making you a sharper thinker (and keeping you that way).

2. *Your physical health.* Stress is directly or indirectly related to just about every health problem there is, especially cardiovascular issues and autoimmune diseases. Meditation is a proven way to improve conditions caused or worsened by stress, and it even reduces pain by helping to slow your breathing and decrease blood flow to the affected area.

3. *Your Emotional Wellness.* Therapists recommend it for many disorders from depression to addiction, and regular meditation has been shown to decrease anxiety, fear, and apathy while increasing empathy, compassion, and contentment.

4. *Your immune system.* Tackling stress is always good for your immune system. A study that looked at how a group of meditators and non-meditators responded to the flu vaccine actually found that the meditator group had more antibodies to the vaccine, indicating stronger immune functioning.

5. *Your ambition.* Meditation boosts creativity, moral reasoning, listening, decision-making, and problem-solving skills—like, all of the things you need to get ahead—at work and in life.

All that said, I get the skepticism; I do. I heard about meditation so much from various CEOs that I actually looked it up to make sure "meditation" was what I thought it was. *They are just talking about sitting in silence, right?* I thought. *What am I missing?* I pictured someone meditating: sitting cross-legged on the floor with their thumbs and middle fingers together, still, silent—and probably really fucking bored. Remember when you were a kid and sitting in silence like that was a punishment? We called it "time-out." And now apparently you can pay two dollars for an app to guide you through the process of sitting in silence, or twenty dollars for a "class" at a studio . . . to sit in silence with a bunch of strangers. Why would I waste my money and time? Meditation seemed like a scam.

Well, it turns out that I was missing a lot. For one thing, I saw meditation as a passive activity, but I learned the hard way that meditation is not passive at all; it's one of the most active, disciplined mental exercises you can take on. Meditation isn't so much about sitting in silence; it's about sitting with *yourself* and being in control of that silence.

After hearing Super Woman after Super Woman praise the benefits of meditating, I finally accepted that, in order to be successful, I needed to get down with gettin' down (on the floor, that is). *If it's a skill that I can learn, for free, and it's going to give me an edge, then I'm going to be the best damn meditator since Buddha,* I thought.

So, I did what any overachiever would do: I bought a bunch of books about meditation, downloaded a bunch of apps to guide me through it, and looked up a bunch of studios to try.

And . . . I totally missed the point. I overthought it. The whole point of meditating is *clearing* your thoughts. It's freeing your mind of the constant assault of thoughts so that you can harness your full mental capacity for other more meaningful and productive pursuits. Instead of clearing my mind, I was filling it up with thoughts about how to get an A+ in meditating.

Meditation isn't something to slay, it's something to practice, which is why some even call it a "practice." It's like going to the gym, except instead of working out your triceps, you are working the part of your brain that aids in mental focus. And, no, you don't need incense or a yoga mat. (Although if those things will help you to get in a zone, then by all means go for it. You do you.) You can do it for free, with no equipment, and just a few minutes a day will reap huge benefits.

Come On, Get Appy

SUPER WOMAN TIP

It might feel counterintuitive to start getting into meditation through a, um, screen, but if you're not sure where to start, there are lots of great apps out there to help you practice this skill in a way that's more structured than just sitting there and attempting to get your Zen on solo. Calm, Headspace, and 10% Happier all offer free trials to help you get into a groove before ramping up into a subscription for more customizable meditation options.

PICK YOUR CHILL PILL

There are two basic types of meditation. One involves focusing on something specific, like a word, an image, or your breath. The other type is about *not* focusing on any one thing—instead, you simply observe your experience and your thoughts moment to moment, without judgment, and stay in the present. If the second type sounds familiar, well, that's because we had a whole step about pretty much this very thing: this is "mindfulness meditation."

In both types of meditation, whenever your attention wanders—you realize you are thinking about the past or worrying about the day to come instead of focusing on your breath or noticing the present—you just direct it back where it belongs. And then repeat.

That's it. No, really. There is no special tool or magical incantation required. Meditation can be guided—where you listen to a voice directing your attention to different parts of your body, etc.—or solo. You can meditate for twenty minutes or five and see huge mental benefits pretty much right away: increased level of focus, decreased anxiety, greater productivity. And you can do it anywhere. I've been known to meditate for a minute or two before going on national television, lights, camera, and all . . . so I mean *anywhere*.

SUPER WOMAN TIP

Mental Floss

Just like brushing and flossing your teeth, maintaining your mental hygiene should be an integral part of your daily routine. And, apologies to Dr. Jennie Jablow (my super successful dentist, who also built a teeth whitening empire), but I would rather have a sparkling brain than a sparkling smile. Neglecting your teeth can lead to yucky things like tooth decay and bad breath (ew), but neglecting your brain can lead to way worse: lack of focus, lagging productivity, and a general failure to make the most of your own brainpower potential. But, since we were never taught proper brain maintenance, we have to come up with our own system. A simple way to start is to practice mindfulness meditation as you brush your teeth in the morning and at night: Don't think about what groceries you need to buy or what some jerk wrote on your last Facebook post or whatever, just really focus on brushing your teeth. Yes, the bristles. The water. The mintiness. Zen out for those few minutes and clean your mind of everything but cleaning your teeth. Boom. You just meditated!! (And made Dr. Jablow happy at the same time.) Now *that's* something to smile about.

There are infinite ways to meditate. You can plop down and listen to a guided meditation with your headphones on and eyes closed. Or, you can more mindfully do something you already enjoy, like go for a run. Ballerina Super Woman Misty Copeland views her morning ballet class as her meditation.

It wasn't until I found what worked for me—learning and practicing a new skill involving repetitive motions—that I became a true believer. It turns out that, when you're learning a new skill, it commands all of your focus, which forced me to be mindful. I found that it also helped to take a class with an instructor or guide first, so that when I did each new activity on my own, I could just let my mind settle on the task at hand rather than whether or not I was doing it right. Here are some of the classes I've taken, which did not fall under the "wellness" category but turned out to be pretty meditative:

- Tomahawk throwing
- Glassblowing
- Beekeeping
- Rock climbing
- Dream catcher making

As long as you keep your mind on what you're doing and return your attention if it wanders, almost any activity can function as meditation. And just like taking different fitness classes besides the usual, like kickboxing/Zumba/spinning (hello, pole dancing!), can make you feel more engaged and motivated to stay in shape, exploring different classes that felt meditative to me kept me excited to keep at keeping my brain in shape.

Apparently, finding meditation in nontraditional places has worked for Angelina Jolie, too. The actress and humanitarian once stated, "I find meditation in sitting on the floor with the kids coloring for an hour, or going on the trampoline." What she said.

CONFESSIONS
OF A SUPER WOMAN

Pouring My Heart Out

"I can't wait to make a heart," I said energetically to Brandon, the coffee barista trainer, waving the foaming wand in front of me like a sword. "Maybe even a bird? I've seen those, too! And then we can have a competition at the end?"

"Slow down, Sparky. We've only got two hours—I doubt you'll even master steaming the milk. It takes our baristas at least fifty hours of training to pour the perfect latte," Brandon told me as he arranged fifteen bottles of almond milk on the chef's table inside his training kitchen.

"Seriously?" I asked. I walked over to the super-duper deluxe espresso machine as if I was approaching a chalkboard full of long division.

"Seriously."

Over the next two hours, I poured and attempted (and failed) to steam enough almond milk to feed a small vegan nation. But Brandon the barista was right. No latte art. Not even a great latte. Just lots of spilled milk.

Still, I got into a rhythm. Pouring the almond milk into the stainless steel frother. Inserting the wand, steadying my hand, and watching the froth rise to the top. Mulling the dark coffee grounds into the espresso maker. Pouring the froth onto the espresso at the bottom of the mug. Repeat. Those two hours flew by as I focused on the singular task at hand: my attempt to master the latte.

I've always had mad respect for baristas who make pretty designs in the foam, but now I truly bow down to their skills. A picture-perfect contrast of brown froth to white froth requires some serious choreography—and my timing was terrible.

As Brandon poured the final demonstration, he said, "Just remember, the faster you pour it, the more momentum the milk has. But if you pour too quickly, it all mixes together out of control. And if you pour too slowly, the foam gets trapped on the surface and doesn't spread out properly."

This felt like a perfect analogy for my life. At times, I had lived it too quickly. Other times—usually after one of the "too quickly" periods had worn me out—I had lived it too slowly. The trick was to find the perfect balance between those two speeds. The perfect latte.

"Here's the heart you wanted," Brandon said, showing me the perfect foam heart he had just poured into my mug.

I had been so focused on getting the milk and foam to the right consistency that I'd totally forgotten about my plan to make a heart. "You win," I said, wiping up the milky mess that had gone everywhere.

"It's not a competition," said Brandon. "It's just a latte."

TRANSCEND, GIRLFRIEND

Years ago, I came up with my own mantra: "There will be time." It's a line from one of my favorite poems, "The Love Song of J. Alfred Prufrock" by T. S. Eliot. I've said it over and over to myself a million times—and have it on the "second tattoo ideas" short list—to remind myself to slow down and take a deep breath. (BTW, my first tattoo was a small semicolon on my wrist, reminding me that there is no hard stop, or period, to my story; a lot of it has yet to be written.) There will be time for the many things I want to do in this life, and most of all, there will be time for *me*.

The word "mantra" is Sanskrit, derived from "*man*," which means "mind," and "*tra*," which means "tool"—so it's literally "tool of the mind." The practice of repeating your mantra to yourself is not just about helping to clear your thoughts, it also helps you train your mind. You use it while meditating or just to center yourself throughout the day.

Believe it or not, people spend money—and lots of it—on coming up with and crafting their mantras. Have you ever heard someone say they do "TM"? It stands for "Transcendental Meditation," a practice during which you are assigned an "exclusive" mantra just for you—to the tune of $1,000. Fans of TM include Super Women like Gwyneth Paltrow and Madonna. I'm not one to judge what you splurge on, but if you're not rolling in Goop or Madge money, then it feels like a lot of cash to spend on something you could easily come up with on your own. You can pick a word that doesn't have any associations or triggers for you, like they do in TM, or pick a phrase like I did. It can be a snippet from your favorite song lyric or a single word that you like. It doesn't even have to be a real word; it could be more of a sound, like "om." Or "nama-slay."

Repeating my mantra to myself is a lot healthier than spouting some of my old favorite phrases, like "I'm so slammed I barely know my own name." I used to wear my "booked solid" and "busy" badges of honor like they just came off the runway. But we determined that those are out of style in Step 6. If you're still sporting yours, take that shit to Goodwill stat. Clear your mind like you would your closet, so you can go shopping for all the best new stuff.

MINDCRAFTING

Once you've cleared your mind, it's important to fill it meticulously. The highest achievers recognize the superpower of their mindset. What you think and how you talk to yourself frames your view of the world and often becomes a self-fulfilling prophecy. So, what are you saying to yourself?

Don't look at me like that. C'mon, we all talk to ourselves! In fact, we say three hundred to one thousand words *per minute* to ourselves. These words are comprised of subliminal commands, guiding us through the motions of our day; reactions to what's happening around us; and judgments of our own actions. And those words can make all the difference. In fact, US Special Forces and Navy SEALS teach positive self-talk as a way of getting through tragedy and hardship in war zones. It's *that* effective.

The body hears everything your mind is saying. Talking to yourself influences your neurobiological response to the current situation, meaning that your mind affects your body and your body affects your mind.

FYI

There will always be people ready to doubt you and point out your flaws, but you don't have to be one of them and shame yourself. Don't play devil's advocate. Be your biggest cheerleader, and when things don't go as planned, talk to yourself the way you would your best friend. I am pretty sure if she told you she made a mistake at work, you wouldn't respond with "You never do anything right," but that's the kind of thing we often say to ourselves.

Start talking to yourself like you would someone you love (because you do, duh). In general, nix words like "always," "never," "worst," "ever," and other extremes from your inner monologue; they're counterproductive and usually, well, wrong. Do you really *always* get lost? Are you really the *worst* at chess? If you take the time to think about it, you'll realize that those extreme statements are rarely true. And if they aren't, don't put them out in the universe to become true.

SO YOU WANNA BE A MENTALIST?

Sometimes ruminating thoughts overrun our brains. You become obsessed with some event, thought, or emotion, and it runs over and over inside your head, getting in the way of . . .

everything else. It can feel like you have one foot on the gas and one on the brake, unable to go anywhere.

If you are having trouble getting your thoughts out of a rut, don't focus on getting rid of the thought itself. Instead, try to tease out the *belief* behind it. And one of the best ways to do that is through old-fashioned journaling. Years of psychological research can be summed up like this: your beliefs about yourself turn into your thoughts, and those thoughts turn into your feelings, which then become your behaviors and actions.

This flowchart has helped me more than any graph I had in school:

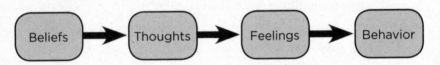

If I'm trying to change something I'm doing, like a destructive behavior or unproductive rumination, I really sit with this chart. For example, when I turned thirty, I started freaking out that my boyfriend hadn't proposed. And during that time, I didn't exactly act with the kindness befitting a Super Woman toward him (or, more importantly, toward myself). And why was that? Sure, I wanted to get married—but was that the root cause of all the drama? No.

Here's how I used my handy flowchart to reverse engineer it:

Behavior: I acted in a way I wasn't proud of by being irritable and picking fights all the time.

Feelings: I felt angry, sad, abandoned, unloved, and afraid.

Thoughts: "I'm not good enough" and "I'm scared I'm going to die alone."

Belief: I need a man to be complete and happy because I need to make right the family situation that went wrong for me as a child. Rewriting my own story means doing the opposite of what I experienced and creating the family I never had.

I didn't need to enroll in anger management classes—I needed to change that core belief about myself. So, I decided on a new belief I wanted to replace it with:

New Belief: I don't need a man to be happy and complete. I'm not responsible for righting past wrongs.

Really focusing on that new belief would go on to change my subsequent thoughts, feelings, and actions in a less superficial, more sustainable way than just trying to change my behaviors. My new, positive, self-affirming belief transformed me into a more positive, self-affirming person (and, eventually, a better partner, too). I went through this same process with other core beliefs to cultivate more positive thoughts. Once I did that, I was ready to kick out the negative thoughts living for free inside my head and confidently raise the rent.

By flowcharting, I traced my lack of positive thinking back to a lack of confidence. This is where negative thoughts come from for many of us, especially women. And confidence is super important for Super Women, especially in the workplace. Confident interviewees have a leg up while job hunting. And once you have that job, bosses tend to assume that more confident employees are more competent as well.

Strike a Pose

SUPER WOMAN TIP

Researchers at Columbia University found that assuming a "power pose" for as little as two minutes makes people feel more confident and in control, and it even changes their hormone levels. A power pose is one that is expansive and takes up space—for example, standing with your hands on hips, chest out, and placing your feet shoulder width apart. Try taking a power position before your next presentation or job interview; it's a trick lots of boss Super Women swear by.

In order to project confidence, you have to feel it. You can meditate every day to build your brain up, but if you spend all your nonmeditating hours tearing yourself down, you'll never rise up. Success won't make you confident. But self-confidence will make you successful. The most effective way I found to increase my self-confidence was to flip my internal script from one that was self-loathing to one that was self-empowering, like this:

Scene 1: You are looking for a job.
Script: "I could never get that position. I'm not qualified, so I'm not going to even waste time applying."

Flip the script: "I know I'm good at what I do and I'm a quick learner, so I'm going to give it a try."

Scene 2: You are envious of someone in a higher position than you.
Script: "She has access to people and resources that I don't, so I could never do what she's doing."
Flip the script: "I'm sure she struggles with responsibilities and prioritizing, too. I'm going to concentrate on my own work today."

Scene 3: You are having a problem at work.
Script: "I don't know what to do here. It's just not my day; I can't catch a break."
Flip the script: "I am in control of this situation. I am in control of myself. I'm going to finish the task at hand before I move on to the next one."

All award-winning scripts go through rewrites. Honor the first edition, even as you write the next. Even the best stories begin with a first draft. And most super heroines aren't born that way—they transform.

MANIFEST DESTINY, CHILD

Another critical part of your new and improved mindset is also one of my favorite words to say: "manifestation." The idea behind manifesting is simple: you want something, you ask for it. Putting your goals and desires out in the universe (or, on the internet, as in the case of Pinterest) and keeping them front and center in your consciousness helps make them happen.

Do you have a Pinterest board loaded with all of the stuff you covet? Clothes, home decor, maybe even that "secret" board with sparkly engagement rings? Yeah, I think a lot of us do. That's because it, along with newer apps to help you vision board, has become the modern way to "manifest" what you want out of life.

You can manifest anything, as long as it's something generally within your control. There's no point in trying to manifest world peace or your boss into liking you more or a dude into being more romantic (as lovely as that would be). You can't change people through manifestation or force someone to do what you want them to do. The only business you can control is yours, so make sure that's what you're all over.

Do you want a career with longevity? A sick car? A sweet pad? A pony? You do you, but decide what it is you want, and then say those words OUT LOUD to yourself. In the shower, in the car, on the treadmill—everywhere. Then say them again. And again.

Keep it short and simple. And put the target of your manifestation in the affirmative. So, instead of saying "I don't want to be broke and homeless," say "I want financial security." Rather than saying "I don't want to fail," say "I want to be the most super version of myself." Remove words like "not," "but," "either," "as well as," or any other modifiers. You aren't settling. There's no "I want to be a Super Woman, but if I can't be, I will settle for just being an Okay Woman." Nope. Super Women don't settle.

Using that as an example, here's how you would manifest becoming a Super Woman:

First, come up with a manifestation. Think of it as your slogan, tagline, or mini motivational speech. You can make it as poetic as you want to, but it's best to keep it simple, straightforward, and affirmative, like "I am a Super Woman" or "I can and I will."

Second, be all about that manifestation. Tweet it, pin it, scream it, sing it, write it. Tattoo it on your body (joking, unless you want to . . .). Do all the things that can be done with your version of "I am a Super Woman." Feel that you are worthy of being a Super Woman every time you say it and think it. Feel those superpowers shooting out from the tips of your toes up through the top of your head. (BTW, Lady Gaga is a fan of manifestations, too. Hers is "Music is my life," and she repeats it to herself every single day.)

Third, visualize what you want. Yes, short and sweet is good, but don't be vague about what you want. It can sound vague to someone else, but if what you want is to be a Super Woman, you better have a clear picture in your head of exactly what that looks like for you. And once you have that picture . . . picture it. Visualization is powerful—studies have found that imagining an activity activates the brain in a way similar to actually performing that activity. That's why so many athletes use visualization to supercharge their performance.

Fourth, make karma your bitch. Karma essentially means that what you do affects what happens to you. You do bad stuff, bad stuff will happen to you. So if you want good stuff, do good stuff. What do you want as a Super Woman? Money? So give money away. Tip more. Donate.

Give to those in need. Give whatever you can and it will come back to you. If that seems far-fetched, think of these examples: If you want friends who have your back, go out of your way to have other people's backs. If you want career success, take the time to mentor and help out others in your industry. I hate clichés, but it's true: what goes around comes around. Including the good stuff that you *want* knockin' on your door.

Disclaimer: manifestation is not magic. You can have all your vibes and juju and hopes and energy on point, but you still won't get what you're after if you sit back and expect karma alone to do the heavy lifting. You want an awesome career? All the manifestation in the world won't get you one if you're not checking job listings, getting employment intel from contacts, and generally pounding the pavement.

The point of mastering meditation and reframing your mindset is to give you the power to take control of your thoughts. And the point of manifesting your destiny is to make you feel like you have the power to take control of your future. Feeling empowered makes your manifestation more likely to come true. And I'm all for that, so bitch, don't kill my vibe.

BOTTOM LINE

Conventional Wisdom: Meditation is for yoga-loving, granola-crunching hippies.

Get those meditation stereotypes out of your head. Meditating can be as simple as focusing on the taste of the toothpaste as you brush your teeth before bed. Focus on whatever, wherever, and whenever you want. The more you work your mental muscles, the stronger they will become.

Conventional Wisdom: There's some *je ne sais quoi* factor to successful people. They are born with a success gene. You either have it or you don't.

Skills of the most successful people are learned, and the successful people I've interviewed have all cited control of their mind as their superpower. As you know by now, your most valuable business asset is not your financial equity or sweat equity. It's your mental equity—does your mind work for you or against you? After all, whether you think you can or you can't, you're right. The space between your ears can be either your greatest asset or your greatest liability. You decide.

Conventional Wisdom: If I want something badly enough, I'll get it eventually.

Any good lawyer needs to know the law to have a chance to win her case, but no one can predict what a jury will decide. If you work your ass off and show up with a positive attitude, you'll have a better chance of winning. But you can't *just* think happy thoughts and expect a winning verdict. Give yourself the best shot for life to rule in your favor by both working and manifesting hard.

STEP
10

FIND YOUR TRIBE
AND LOVE THEM HARD

Super Women Fly Best Together

When I returned home from the hospital after my breakdown, my fridge was stocked, my sheets were clean, and my bed was made better than I could have done it. I didn't know it at the time, but after a few frantic texts, one of my besties drove four hours through the night to be there for me. And when I wasn't allowed visitors, she went to my apartment (as a true bestie, she's always on the "key list" for my building). By the time I got there she had already gone. I only learned of her visit when I returned home to my favorite vegan mac and cheese in the fridge and a tidy apartment, which was a perfect contrast to the mess I had just lived through and exactly what I didn't know I needed. But, she did.

I realized then that the best of friends aren't just the ones you vacation with, or cry about exes with, or who hold your hand in the hospital. The best ones are *all* of those things, sure, but they're also behind the scenes, supporting you in quiet, unsung ways that are entirely unique to you and your needs. They're your rock at rock bottom.

The most successful Super Women not only have their *own* backs, they have a community of other Super Women behind them, too. Emotional Wellness takes a village. In this step, we'll establish who's in yours—and learn how to (gracefully) get those who are bringing you down to move on out.

CREATING A BADASS VILLAGE

Enjoying a tight community (or what the researchers call "social connectedness") is directly related to success. Look back at the goals you came up with in Step 3. Who can you count on to support you on the way to reaching those goals? And who do you want to celebrate with when you get there? And commiserate with if you don't?

Since you are the CEO of your own life, consider the important and influential people who help you run the business of being you as your personal C-suite. The C-suite of a company is made up of all the firm's most important and influential members. It's all the executives who have the word "chief" in their title, as in CEO or "*chief* executive officer," CFO or "*chief* financial officer," CTO or "*chief* technology officer," and so on.

Just like a company looks for different skills in a CFO than it does in a CTO, we look for different qualities in different kinds of relationships. But whatever circle you're moving in, the people making it up should have a few basic squad qualities in common:

- *Validating.* They like you for who you are, and when your confidence slips, they remind you of all the ways you are awesome (and/or encourage you to reread the list you made in Step 2 to remind yourself).

- *Honest.* Being validating doesn't mean agreeing with everything you say—these are the people who care enough about you to tell you the truth, even when it means calling you out on your shit (with love, of course). Their honesty helps keep *you* honest.

- *Consistent.* This doesn't have to mean you text hourly and meet every Friday for drinks. Between time and geography, sometimes your most important people aren't the ones you see most often. But they *are* the ones who consistently have your back and won't front if it's been a minute since you've chatted.

Before you start thinking about who in your life has these qualities, ask yourself: Do *you*? If you are invalidating, dishonest, and inconsistent, why would you expect the people around you to treat you any differently? After all, don't forget you're a member of whatever club you're in—and in this case, you're the CEO, so lead by example.

As they say in many recovery programs, "Keep your side of the street clean." That is, take care of the 50 percent of any relationship that you have control over . . . *yours*. The previous nine steps have helped you do that by getting yourself, your priorities, and your instincts in order so that you're in a better position to be a stellar friend, partner, family member, and colleague. Now, if you're ready to cross the street, let's decide who you want waiting for you on the other side.

WORK PEEPS

I know that you can't choose most of the work people you have in your life, but you *can* choose which of them you invest in. It's important to identify a trusted circle of friends and advocates at work that you'll have for the long run, regardless of where it is you actually work. People leave jobs. They lose jobs. They often end up somewhere else in your industry. And they *always* remember who still talked to and hung out with them during the "hiatus" they had before getting another gig. I will never forget the people who stayed in touch with me when I had nothing immediate that I could "do" for them. Those are the people I do the most for today.

In addition to the basic qualities we talked about, like honesty, here are the three things I look for in professional relationships I want to develop:

1. *Positive attitude.* Would you want to foster a relationship with a Debbie Downer? I wouldn't.

2. *Creativity.* I don't just surround myself with wicked smart, creative people in my own industry; I am attracted to creative people in general. It's a good idea to bring work peeps from outside your industry into your inner circle—their ideas about what they do might spark a new approach to what you do.

3. *Straight shooter.* If I invest time in a work relationship, I don't want to waste it on the phony formalities often associated with work decorum. I'm not saying you have to do actual shots with this person, but I like to surround myself with people who don't have

their guard totally up and are able to keep it real—at work and elsewhere.

What you look for in your important work relationships is up to you. Maybe you list power or expertise as qualities you want in your work tribe. Maybe you just want to invest in influential executives above you so you can jockey for a promotion behind the scenes. Remember, it's totally fine to value whatever you value, not what you *think* you should value, as long as it is in alignment with your *true* truth. If you value power and influence, it's not fine to pretend like you don't.

And because I'm a straight shooter, I'll tell it to you like it is, even if what I'm about to say isn't popular: Getting ahead at work *is* a popularity contest. And that's not necessarily a bad thing. Studies have shown time and again that people with more allies at the office perform better at work, and people with a larger contact list get ahead faster, gaining bigger and more regular promotions than their lone she-wolf counterparts. One Gallup poll found that people who had a work bestie were 43 percent more likely to receive recognition and praise for their work in a given week. And a LinkedIn study found that 46 percent of workers worldwide believe that work friends are important to their overall happiness. There can be salary benefits as well because discussing personal matters like how much you make with work confidantes provides valuable insights into your company or industry's compensation—so you can ask for what you deserve. Could you price your house to sell without knowing the price of comparable homes in the area? Sure. But will it be better valued, and more likely to sell, with that information in hand? Abso-fucking-lutely.

At the end of the (work)day, study after study has shown that the best predictor of team success is not smarts or effort—it's how team members feel about one another. When that feeling is positive, everyone succeeds. So, the ultimate goal for your work relationships is not *just* to be popular, it's to make positive connections. While much has been written about the power of "weak ties" at work, or more transactional interactions, I believe in the superpower of "strong ties," or more meaningful and long-lasting ones. And even though it seems counterintuitive, the best way to do that is by *not* talking about work.

CONFESSIONS
OF A SUPER WOMAN

Hi, My Name Is . . .

Around the time my work obsession started to peak, after I'd moved to NYC to start my dream gig at CNBC, I scored an invite to a secret influencer dinner series. The doors opened on a beautiful Upper West Side apartment, flooded with lights from huge windows that faced the Hudson River. I politely took off my shoes as our host gave me the "rules" for the evening—and realized I'd had no idea what I'd gotten myself into.

The biggest rule was this: No talking about—or even mentioning—what you do for work. Like, at all. And, even if you recognized someone, you had to basically pretend you didn't until the end of the evening (which was pretty difficult, considering that one of the guests was, um, Bill Nye, the Science Guy).

While we *weren't* talking about what we did for a living, we'd all be cooking dinner together. It was Mexican night, and the large kitchen was divided into little "stations"—one for preparing guacamole, one for chopping veggies, etc. Once everyone had arrived, we rotated through each station in a way that ensured everyone there got a chance to talk to everyone else. Unable to talk about work, I found myself really struggling to continue the conversation once I'd exhausted the story of the avocado tree I'd had in my backyard growing up. (Yes, I was the captain of the guacamole station.)

When dinner was ready, we all sat down to eat the meal we had worked together to prepare. At that point, we went around the table person by person, everyone else guessing what each member of the group did for a living based on the conversations we had about everything *but* work. And after everyone else had a chance to guess, we finally revealed our actual job.

The group had been curated by the host, a notable behavioral scientist who got off (intellectually) on watching how we handled ourselves within the evening's strict parameters. He was the only person who knew everyone's profession ahead of time. As we would soon discover, we were a varied bunch. Besides the Science Guy, and myself, there was an editor-in-chief of a major magazine, a famous comedian, and an acclaimed architect, among others.

After dinner was over, we gathered in the kitchen again, this time to wash the many dishes. And in a super weird turn of events, especially with this high-powered crowd and in this high-powered city, everyone went back to the non-work-related conversations we'd been having before the big jobs reveal. Just as weird, I found myself loosening up, too. We laughed hard, sang badly, and even learned how to saber a bottle of champagne (don't try it at home, kids). I remember bringing up something job related to a woman it turned out I had actually worked with before but never met, and the conversation seemed almost inappropriate. Everyone there was at the peak of a demanding career, but no one was spending the night on their phone making deals. Instead, the group of us enjoyed being silly and telling stories, developing friendships that lasted longer and were the more meaningful for it.

Every time I meet someone now, I think of that night. Of course, after the "Hi, my name is . . ." part of an introduction is over, "What do you do?" is usually the default first question. That part hasn't changed but my response to it has.

Recently, I met someone at a happy hour hosted by a financial company who quickly, after introducing herself, asked, "Where are you from?" I didn't skip a beat and answered, "Los Angeles." Everyone around me started laughing. They said that the woman was asking where I was from as in "What company are you from?" I laughed and she asked again, "So, where are you from?" This time I said, "Los Angeles, where are you from?"

Before I set out on my pursuit to become a Super Woman, I lived for the "What do you do?" and "What are you working on?" questions because I felt like work defined me. You wanna know more about me, outside of what I do for a living? Too bad; here's another work thing I'm doing. I relied solely on my professional accomplishments to build professional contacts. And while I had "connections," I didn't build any meaningful connections.

As Super Women, no job title or occupation could possibly define all that we are, anyway. The "hows" of what we do—where we've been, the struggles and triumphs we face, the adventures we have—are so much more interesting. That's the stuff that resonates with people. Own that narrative and you'll own your next dinner party, too.

If you find yourself struggling to have something more than work to talk about, there's a good chance your "joy bucket" that we talked about in Step 6 is empty and it's time to fill it back up. How you describe yourself to others reveals a lot about how you see yourself and where you're focusing your energy. I now use these "introducing myself" moments as a litmus test to see if I'm in need of a mental tune-up. If it's hard for me to carry on a conversation about my personal adventures and misadventures as of late, then I know it's time to have more of them.

Even if you're in a work environment, it's okay *not* to talk about work. In fact, those conversations are often most memorable and create the strongest connections. When I take on new projects or hires, I care less about the PowerPoint presentations and more about the connection. You better believe I will remember and care more about a woman who told me a story about going hiking in Patagonia or learning how to grow tomatoes on her balcony than whatever someone else said about their last company or first internship. Be honest with yourself: you'd rather listen to other people's stories, right? (I mean you've been listening to mine this whole time.) But, also be ready to tell your own. And, if you're starved for anything to say, maybe it's time to flip back to Step 4 and make sure you're not missing a slice of the pie. By now, you should have plenty of other big pieces that fill you up.

YOUR PROFESSIONAL POSSE

A Super Woman knows what she doesn't know—but also knows how to find someone who does and then ask them for help. We surround ourselves with all kinds of experts. These are the people who, while you may not call them in a crisis, enable you to pursue your goals. That might mean your kids' nanny, your assistant, or your handy neighbor who can fix anything. It's your posse, so make it what you want, but here are a few examples of experts you might want to add:

> *Mentor.* This is someone you admire professionally and aspire to learn from. Ideally, they work in the same or a similar industry as you, but not at your actual company. They have your best interests in mind as a professional and as a person, and you can rely on them for nonbiased feedback about your career choices and trajectory. The key here is that this is an actual relationship, which you take the time to grow and foster—without expecting anything concrete in return. (Advice and guidance when you need it? Yes. A big connection or actual job offer? No.) Also, get the idea out of your head that a mentor has to be older. I consider my friends Randi Zuckerberg and Daphne Oz to be my mentors, and they are basically my

age. Randi does a lot of the same things I do, but in the technology space, and Daphne does a lot of what I do in the food space. While industry veterans can be helpful for giving you the general lay of the land, I'm also a big advocate of "peer mentors"—those who are more familiar with the type of work and contracts you might be getting now, in the present day, not just twenty years ago. Start your search for peer mentors on LinkedIn by seeing who you might already be connected to within your industry, and then reach out to see if they'd be open to meeting.

Therapist. Going to a therapist is like going to a trainer for your brain. You definitely don't need to have a diagnosed mental illness to go. In fact, *everyone* should go. (But if you do have something going on, it's doubly important.) My long-time psychiatrist is Lucy. I find this hilarious and fitting because I played the character "Lucy" in my grade school production of *You're a Good Man, Charlie Brown.* My scene was the one where Lucy opens a neighborhood psychiatry booth—you know, the one where she puts up a little handwritten sign for whether the doctor is "in" or "out." Having this real-life Lucy has literally saved my life. But while the Lucy in the play charged five cents for her services, mine charges five thousand times that. Seriously. I fully recognize that I am nothing but lucky to be able to afford my Lucy. But there are ways to find *your* Lucy without the sticker shock (which I outline in the Resources section in the back of the book).

Life coach. If you have the cash to lock down a life coach, this can be a great person to include in your inner circle.

If I asked an executive ten years ago who had had the greatest impact on her career, the typical answers were "my college professor" or "my first boss." Now I hear "life coach" or even "spiritual advisor" way more often. A life coach might be someone you bring into your circle later in life, once you have the resources to spend on one; or you might also decide that, financial commitment or not, it's just not for you. Either way, there are life coaches who specialize in everything from ADHD to career issues to creativity. Many household-name executives have turned to different types of coaches and advisors throughout their careers:

- **Oprah Winfrey:** Oprah has attributed some of her career success—you know, that media empire—to her life coach, Martha Beck, with whom she has worked for years. As a result of her own personal experience, Oprah has been a major advocate for life coaching, regularly bringing various specialists on her show and encouraging her audience to bring on a life coach to get ahead.
- **Steve Jobs:** The Apple founder employed thousands of people but often listened to no one—except for a Japanese-born Zen master named Kobun Chino Otogawa. Jobs officially brought him on as a company "spiritual advisor." Kobun presided over Jobs' wedding and also influenced much of his design work and philosophy.
- **Serena Williams:** She may not be an executive, per se, but as one of the highest-paid athletes out there—male or female—she is definitely the boss.

When she started to come up against injuries that kept her off the tennis court, she worked with the one and only Tony Robbins to remain focused and train through her injuries. Did it work? Well, let's just say she has the Grand Slam victories to prove it.

Talking about getting help from people outside of the usual support system has become more accepted and therefore more popular. From Silicon Valley to Wall Street to Washington, the stigma of talking about shrinks and spirituality has been replaced with story swapping and contact sharing.

ROMANTIC RELATIONSHIPS

Choosing the right partner is more important than choosing the right job, because even as career opportunities come and go, your ride or die—if it's the right one—will be the person supporting you through the whole journey (sometimes in more ways than one). Your partner should be your head cheerleader, validating your ambitions and supporting your career no matter what. I wrote a lot about this in *Boss Bitch*. At first, my editor said, "Lapin, this is a business book. Business books don't talk about love and family planning." And I said: "Exactly."

Choosing the *wrong* partner can send your Emotional Wellness into a tailspin. Stress and anxiety impacts everything, especially your performance at work—and that includes stress of the romantic variety. I mean, when you're going through a breakup, are you able to focus on work? Um, no. If the breakup was bad enough, there are probably days you are just happy to be able to focus your eyes on your computer screen.

Now obviously this category of your tribe is super-duper

personal, but I'll share a few things that I look for in a romantic partner. For the sake of this book's thesis, let's focus on the "need to have" qualities because those will affect your Emotional Wellness way more than "nice to have" qualities or physical characteristics like piercing blue eyes. Here's what I look for in a S-U-P-E-R man:

- *Secure.* I'm talking about the emotional, not the financial kind of security here. "Attachment theory" says that people have one of three main attachment styles: secure, insecure, and avoidant. The names are pretty self-explanatory. Insecure and avoidant people are the worst for each other and secure people won't tolerate anything else. It's taken me a long time to feel like I am secure in my approach to relationships, and I want to be with someone else who is as well.
- *Understanding.* My life can get chaotic. I don't mind a little drama (or "passion," which is a common euphemism for it) outside my relationship, but I don't want that volatility inside it. Having a stable partner is important because it stops me from catastrophizing a situation.
- *Principled.* I'm not perfect but my principles are rock solid. I want the same from my dude. We don't need to agree on everything (who does?) but we do need to share core values for the life we live now and the life we want to build, together.
- *Educated.* This doesn't mean in a book-smart sense. I value emotional and street smarts over anything someone might have learned in a classroom anyway. To me, being educated is more about being curious

than well-read: collecting adventures and using them to shape your view on the world.

- *Romantic.* A lot of what I need, I can do for myself, but this is one thing I can't have on my own (I like myself, I don't like myself *that* much). Romance and sexual chemistry are musts in this person, otherwise they would be in another part of my crew. Frida Kahlo said it best: "Take a lover who looks at you like maybe you are magic."

To be clear, "need to have" qualities are different than needing someone. Your partner should support you but should never be the only thing holding you up. Codependency happens when you are reliant on a relationship and your partner's approval for your own sense of worth or identity. If you are feeling this way, ask yourself, "How empty must I be to be so full of someone else?" Then, focus on filling your self-worth back up. Remember: you can't pour from an empty cup.

FAMILY

Your family, if you're lucky enough to have one, can be your foundation. The best part of having a healthy family is that no one quite knows you like they do. But if your relationship with them is strained or just nonexistent, staying apart might be even better.

I included "family" here because I know that it's a common category for many people, but the fact is that, for me, my close friends *are* my family. Sometimes having the same moral DNA is a stronger bond than having the same blood. After my parents' bitter divorce and my father's death from an overdose, I became estranged from my mother and brother; it was a lot on all of us and, honestly, enforcing the boundaries between myself and my dysfunctional family is critical for my well-being. I used to be embarrassed to talk about it, and I felt like I was alone in doing it. Of course, I'm not. Countless Super Women like Jennifer Aniston, Adele, Kate Hudson, and Meghan Markle are estranged in some way from their families. It's not always pretty or easy but as Jeannette Walls writes in *The Glass Castle*, one of my favorite memoirs of all time, "everyone who is interesting has a past."

Maybe you come from a secure, supportive family, and you can't imagine leaving them out of your village. Great, add 'em! Or maybe you come from a tough home life and know *exactly* what I'm talking about (in which case, I feel for you, sister). Regardless of whether yours is a happy one or doesn't exist at all, all families are complicated. But no matter what, your family isn't exempt from the boundaries you set for yourself back in Step 5, and the fact that they are family doesn't mean you have to have them in your inner circle. If they are, it should be because that's what you've chosen.

CLOSE FRIENDS

It's often said that "friends are your chosen family." In Japanese, the term "*kenzoku*" means "family," but it doesn't just refer to blood relatives; it also includes friends. I cherish my *kenzoku*. But, choosing them once doesn't mean you have to keep choosing them in perpetuity.

I don't need to tell you that friends come and go. Some of my childhood friends have come back into my life after a long absence; I guess it's the strong bond we formed back when our middle school world seemed as dramatic as an episode of *Dawson's Creek*. Other friends, both from childhood and more recent times, I've lost touch with and likely will never see again.

According to psychology, there are a few factors that make people stick together:

1. *History.* You might have nothing in common, but you shared an experience or went through a period of time together. Especially when it's something traumatic (ahem, like middle school), that bond is strong.

2. *Shared interests and values.* You like the same things. You have the same sense of humor. You have plenty to talk about, and it is easy to think of something to do together.

3. *Equality.* You both are equally invested in the relationship, and also equally independent (and not dependent on each other or codependent, aka you both need someone to need you). If one person is more dependent on the other, the relationship is imbalanced and can feel like a losing game of tug-of-war.

If only one out of these three things is present, it's likely the relationship will not last. Think about it: if you have history but one person is overly dependent on the other and/or you have nothing in common, weathering long-term storms is going to be pretty tricky. At least two—but probably three—factors are necessary to have a lasting and beneficial bond. So who are your "people"? This might feel a little callous as you determine who makes the cut. Don't forget: you have no obligation to anyone, no matter who they are and how you met, who treats you badly or doesn't serve your greater good.

Bye, Felicias

Like your internet browser, if you open too many tabs at once, you're going to crash. You only have so much bandwidth. Don't waste it on shitty people.

Building a new super life will cost you your old habits and behaviors, many of which stem from bad relationships. I've had to make some hard cuts and sever some toxic, albeit longstanding, ties. And I came to realize that doing so was not an act of cruelty, but an act of self-care. Extracting yourself from relationships that are dragging you down will free up mental capacity you can use to focus on building those that raise you up.

How to Rid Your Life of Toxic People

You can tell a lot about a person by answering this simple question: How do I feel after I see so-and-so?

If your answer is anything other than "fan-fucking-tastic," then buh-bye, so-and-so. Now, there are exceptions to this rule, like being there for a good friend who might just be going through a particularly shitty time (and acting like it). But as Super Woman Amy Poehler once said, "Anybody who doesn't make you feel good, kick them to the curb. And the earlier you start in your life, the better."

Here are five surefire ways to tell if someone is polluting your life:

1. *They're a drain on energy.* If you dread seeing this person, or feel totally depleted after you do, they are not additive to your life. They are toxic.

2. *They're a drain on resources.* Anyone who regularly exploits your generosity—whether it's your time or actual money—is not a friend but a freeloader.

3. *They're all about the drama.* Think drama just follows some people around? False. Toxic people attract negative energy, which makes them a magnet for drama. Time for a curtain call.

4. *You feel the need to make excuses for them.* If you find yourself making excuses for how someone behaves or treats you or others, first of all, stop, because you are enabling them and thus part of the problem; and second of all, recognize them for what they are: a negative force in your and others' lives.

5. *They make You less You.* This is perhaps the scariest one of all. If you find that you are your judgiest, meanest, or most insecure self around this person, they're not a friend. True friends make you shine brightest. Toxic people turn out the lights.

Often, toxic friendships dissolve on their own. People are lazy, and maintaining a friendship takes effort, so if you pull away, chances are that your "friend" isn't going to chase you down. But some friends, even bad ones, won't go quietly, and they require more of an actual breakup. If you need to let some people go, for whatever reason, here are my suggestions for making the break:

- *Say nothing.* Where appropriate, that's often the loudest message of them all. Saying nothing isn't literally nothing—if you come into contact with the person, give the most basic response you can.

- *Don't ghost.* Saying nothing is not "ghosting." If someone is regularly blowing up your phone and you're not acknowledging them at all, then that's not cool. If you feel pressured to give an explanation, try something like "I'm taking some time to focus on myself and my priorities." Or "I have a lot going on right now, and won't be able to see you." Done. Repeat that message as often as you need to and, eventually, they'll get the point.

- *Be kind and genuine.* Kindness is super underrated and being kind even to people you no longer want in your life is just the right thing to do. For better or worse, they had an impact on you and contributed to making you the Super Woman you are today. Plus: People change, situations change. Life is long and the world is small. Don't be an asshole. You're likely going to run into some of these people again, especially if they're part of your larger network, and while we may not want those relationships in our lives, we don't want bad juju, either.

Toxic people suck up your precious time (well, they just *suck*, too). And as I've said before, time is hands-down your most valuable asset. You can make more money; you can't make more time. The more protective you are of how to spend it, the stronger your community will be and *you* will be stronger as a result.

Squad Goals

In the same way that we cleared our minds only to fill them with the best, most productive thoughts and actions in the last step, once you clear your friend deck, you'll only want to invite the best, most supportive people onboard. And, yes, you can still make friends as an adult. I have. But, if you feel like it's been a while since you've had to, here are some ways to fill the friend deck back up:

Sign up for classes. I've tried the most random classes, from horticulture to a samba dance class held in a pool. The more I forced myself out of the "Friday night out" or "Sunday brunch" routines, the more I connected with people I wouldn't likely run into at my usual brunch spot. There's a site I love called coursehorse.com that allows you to find and sign up for all kinds of fun classes in one place. Airbnb also offers experiences now, in addition to home rentals. If you have an idea for a class and you can't find it, just call the business directly and see if you can take a lesson with them. I couldn't find a class to help me create the latte art I'd always wanted (and told you about in Step 9), so I called a coffee shop and asked if they would teach me—and they did.

Find free stuff. I've signed up for a bunch of different news-letters that show all of the activities in my neighborhood that are free, many of which I never would have heard of otherwise. An acclaimed chef doing a demonstration at the opening of her new restaurant? A poetry reading? Tai chi in the park? Yes, please.

Join a club. No, clubs are not just for high schoolers trying to get into a good college. I'm sure there are a ton of sports clubs in your area, like softball or kickball leagues, that you could join to feel part of a community and get your sweat on as a bonus. But, beyond that, there are book clubs, language conversation clubs, and groups that get together to talk about just about everything, from Southeast Asian art to weird science. Try Meetup.com for ideas. The ones that meet to talk about stuff you never thought you would have an interest in are the best. Go hang out with those folks. And, if there's no group already formed to talk about what you want, then go ahead and start one yourself!

Rethink your route. Think about how you can replace your inner creature of habit with a creature of curiosity. I try to walk a different street home every day in NYC. Along the way, I've discovered a Samurai sword fighting class, a seminar on Jewish mysticism, and met a cool home-less guy who played chess with me—and, ahem, schooled me—in the park. You don't have to be in a walkable city to change up your route. You can find hidden gems anywhere, but only if you look for them (and not down at your phone).

Talk to everyone. Staring at your shoes or at your phone in an elevator or in line at the grocery store doesn't help you meet new people or find potential adventures. A girlfriend of mine, who I met while we were both eating brunch alone at a counter (I say I picked her up at a bar), has a philosophy called "the hey method." She just says, "hey!" whether it's to a potential business partnership or a cute guy that walks by. The "hey" can end with just that. Or, it can end with a new partnership, a new boyfriend, and new unlikely buddies, like my friend Zamira, whom I met in a boxing class. She and her family fled Cuba, and the stories she told me brought everything I'd read about to life. I've also met a Holocaust survivor and a Special Olympian—just by saying "hey." Take "the hey challenge." Can you say "hey" to one stranger a day? Yes you can.

And yes *we* can. Fun fact: Birds don't fly in formation just because it looks pretty to humans admiring them from below. They fly together because doing so conserves energy; the V shape they form makes the whole group more aerodynamic, cutting through the sky with less effort per bird. It also keeps them safe—it's much harder for larger, predatory birds to take on a flock than it would be to pick off one bird flying solo. Together, in formation, birds are stronger, faster, and go farther. Together.

BOTTOM LINE

Conventional Wisdom: I can take care of myself and I don't need anyone.

You may not "need" anyone, but to reach the heights we both know you're capable of, you should *want* to build a strong network of other Super Women and Super Men with whom to enjoy the view.

Conventional Wisdom: Your family is your family no matter what. You have an obligation to them.

You are a grown-ass woman who is in charge of her own life and how she spends her precious time. The same goes for your best friend from elementary school, the gossipy bitches around the water cooler, and everyone else. People should be in your life because you want them there, and no one—not even your immediate family—has the right to drain your time and energy.

Conventional Wisdom: Making new friends is for grade school; I'm too old for that shit.

If you're not making new friends, mentors, and professional contacts right up until you're an old lady (and hey, as Betty White showed us, old ladies can still make new friends!), then you are seriously missing out. There are lots of ways to build out your squad. Just remember that when people show you who they are, believe them (preach, Maya Angelou!). Otherwise you can—and sometimes you must—kick those toxic friends to the curb.

STEP

11

CHECK YOURSELF

Self-Care Reality Checks, Rituals, and Routines

Checking in with yourself is about first observing. Channel your inner Jane Goodall, the trailblazing anthropologist who produced the world's most important research on primates. Jane didn't go into the jungle and say "good chimpanzee" or "bad chimpanzee." She didn't judge. She observed. And out of those observations came incredible insights not only into primates but into human nature as well. It's in our nature to be curious, so regularly channel that curiosity into checking up on the evolution of your super self.

We stay on top of all kinds of other regular appointments: our monthly mani/pedis, our quarterly work reviews, our yearly pap smears. Staying on top of what makes us Super Women takes just as much—if not more—maintenance. Yet it's not something that shows up on our calendars as often, and if it does, it's likely the first thing to get canceled when your schedule gets chaotic. But here's the thing: life will always have some level of chaos, and caring for yourself is the best way to manage it.

"Life, liberty, and the pursuit of happiness." Note that the Declaration of Independence says we have the right to "the pursuit of happiness" and not just "happiness." That's because happiness itself is not a right or a given but a constant, ongoing process. In this step, I'm going to show you how to check in with yourself on the regular to make sure you're maintaining your Emotional Wellness. And, if you find yourself slipping, I'll tell you the best ways to troubleshoot with self-care routines and rituals so that you get back on track. If you don't want to make the struggle real, you've got to make the pursuit real.

CHECKING IN ON YOURSELF

Making time for your Emotional Wellness is something only you can do. Sure, your tribe of supporters can help you stick to a healthy schedule, but only you can manage your calendar in a way that allows for the practice of self-care every single day. And only you can know if you haven't done that—and if you're starting to feel the effects.

FIVE SIGNS YOU MIGHT NEED A MENTAL HEALTH DAY:

1. *You're anxious.* Maybe you're too worried to concentrate, or you even have physical symptoms like chest tightness, abdominal pain, shortness of breath, or sweaty palms. If you're feeling

particularly uneasy and you're having a hard time snapping out of it, it might be a good day to take some quiet time to yourself to nip a potential anxiety attack in the bud.

2. *You're Miss Testy.* If you're so on edge that you're getting into it with your family, friends, or coworkers for no apparent reason, it could be that your nerves are fried or fired up and you're mentally short circuiting. Spending a day off the grid could unwind some of the aggro tension.

3. *You just can't seem to perk up.* If you've downed a cup of coffee, a latte, iced tea, and green tea, and you're still feeling sluggish, then it's likely time to step away from the hustle *and* the caffeine. When you feel like you're moving in slow motion, take extra care to get hydrated . . . like a whole day minus caffeine and plus eight glasses of water.

4. *You're so tired . . . but you can't sleep.* The part of the brain that interprets our thoughts and feelings is very sensitive to the impact of sleep deprivation. Unfortunately, stress can make it hard to sleep, leaving you exhausted in the morning. Sure, we'd all love another thirty minutes in the AM. That's not a reason for a mental health day, but true exhaustion is.

5. *You're constantly sick.* One day it's the sniffles, the next day it's a headache. Maybe you just can't catch a break when it comes to physical ailments. Or maybe you're running yourself into the ground.

> Taking a breath and a day off will likely do more for
> your immune system than another Z-Pak.

Chronically feeling any one of these things is reason enough to pump the brakes and give yourself time to recalibrate. Of course, it would be nice if checking in with yourself was as simple as shaking a Magic 8 Ball and waiting for the answer to swim to the surface. But just like with an actual Magic 8 Ball, the results aren't always clear. *I just feel . . . off,* you might find yourself thinking. That's your "gut" talking.

But can you trust your gut? If you can't yet, that's okay—your "gut" or "intuition" is not magic, it's a skill that you can work on and improve. Even if you've never thought about it before, you have a head start. Years of research have shown that women typically have stronger intuitive skills than men because, back in the day, we needed them to keep our children alive without thermometers, doctors, and all the medical knowledge we have now. Plus, we've already talked about many of the tools that have been shown to boost your brain's intuitive superpowers, namely mindfulness, meditation, and manifestation from Steps 8 and 9. Continue to strengthen your intuition by paying attention to your body's own signals and trusting that it's in need of extra self-care.

GUT CHECK

Neuroscience shows that our brains do this thing called "chunking"—taking different pieces of information from previous experiences that are similar to the current situation and then guiding us quickly toward a decision. The result is your intuition. It's a complex feeling that actually comes from pattern recognition in your brain. So, to train your gut, you have to train your brain. (Fun fact: in Eastern medicine, your gut is considered your "second brain.")

THREE WAYS TO INVEST IN YOUR INTUITION

1. *Be sensitive to your senses.* Sight, smell, hearing, taste, and touch are the five conventional senses. As you go about your day, take the time to notice all that you can with these five senses. Doing so can heighten your sensitivity to your sixth sense: intuition. This is the sense that runs your current situation against others you've experienced in the past to help you to make an informed choice. So, the more information you gather from your environment, the more your pattern-seeking intuition has to go on.

2. *Test your gut.* Do a little A/B testing of your own. Have a feeling about which duo will get eliminated next from your favorite dance competition show? Getting a sense that it will rain tomorrow even though the weather forecast says it won't? Do you just *know* that creepy guy in accounting is up to no good? Write these feelings or predictions down, then check them later. Were you right or wrong? Try to identify

the factors that led you to make the prediction you did.

3. *Listen to your body.* Your intuition speaks to you through your body, and the more you cultivate awareness of your body—called "somatic awareness"—the more sensitive you become. If you get a distinct physical feeling when you're trying to make a decision, pay attention. Do you feel light or heavy? Have a sick feeling in your gut? Overtaken by chills and goose bumps? Note these inbound messages from your sixth sense and use them to identify the right decisions by looking for the choices that feel right to you.

FYI

Tons of successful people attribute their success to intuition. In fact, the ultimate investing Super Man, Warren Buffett, relies on intuition heavily. He doesn't begin a potential investment by looking at a company's numbers; instead, he follows those companies that resonate with him, and *then* looks at their numbers to make a final decision. Listening to his instincts, he's profited wildly from big swings in the market, investing in companies like Coca-Cola and See's Candies, when others were fearful. Buffett's intuition keeps him away from complicated tech stuff—instead he gravitates toward great American staples that he understands. His philosophy stems from two basic tenets: "know yourself" and "know your business." (And, by "basic tenets," I mean "tenets that made him billions and billions of dollars.")

Similarly, grand masters in chess develop strong intuition about their best next move (and the ten moves after that) only after years of study and practice. They use reason to make sure the move is safe, but they rely first on the intuition they've developed through experience and pattern recognition. After all, there are too many possible moves in chess for it to be played any other way.

The most valuable knowledge you can get from a super strong intuition is an accurate reading of yourself. Learning to trust yourself is about being able to read the board objectively and then thinking ahead. The queen is the most powerful piece on the board—but only if she knows her next move and why she's making it.

TAKE A MENTAL HEALTH DAY

The concept of taking a "mental health day" is pretty widespread, and becoming more and more accepted (it's even legally protected, in most cases, as a totally acceptable reason to take a sick day). But being familiar with the concept isn't the same as embracing it for yourself. Do you ever take a mental health day when you need one? And, if you do, do you tell others that's what it is?

You should. Case in point: A few years back, a woman

in Michigan named Madalyn Parker emailed her boss and coworkers saying, "Hey, team, I'm taking today and tomorrow to focus on my mental health. Hopefully I'll be back next week refreshed and back to 100%."

The *CEO of the company* (granted, it was a small company, but still) wrote her back: "Hey, Madalyn, I just wanted to personally thank you for sending emails like this. Every time you do, I use it as a reminder of the importance of using sick days for mental health—I can't believe this is not standard practice at all organizations. You are an example to us all, and help cut through the stigma so we can bring our whole selves to work."

Madalyn shared the exchange on social media and broke the internet, with people thanking her for being unapologetic and honest about using her personal time for mental health and calling her company's CEO the "Boss of the Year." Hey, I agree. Ben Congleton, you get my vote. But the internet explosion only highlighted the need for more of us to be brave enough to advocate for ourselves.

FYI

You don't have to be a lawyer or consultant to think of yourself as having billable hours. Remember, the personal/vacation days that you take or leave on the table are all part of your overall compensation package. Use this simple equation to figure out just how valuable those mental health days are:

*Your annual salary / Total hours worked
= Your hourly wage*

Notice that the more of your hard-earned days off that you actually take off, the higher that hourly wage climbs.

Ignoring your mental health can be costly for yourself and your career; look at taking a day off when needed as an investment in both. And, if you're a manager, empower those who work with or under you to take the time they need, too. Meg Whitman, the former CEO of eBay and Hewlett-Packard, is one of a growing number of executives who are reminding companies of the importance of providing mental health days, extended insurance coverage for mental health, and more open forums to talk about issues. And that's not just because she's a good person; it's good business. Depression alone, whether situational or chronic, costs US companies an estimated $210 billion a year—yes, BILLION, with a big "B"—half of which is in workplace costs including missed days and reduced productivity and performance.

While all bosses *should* follow Meg and Ben's lead and be open to their employees taking mental health days, I am well aware that many of them are not. The key to asking for a day off is to not be wishy-washy or embarrassed about it. Be assertive about what you need. If you know that asking for a "mental health day" won't go over well, don't fake a cold or lie. Instead, go with "personal reasons." And leave it at that. Your employer cannot ethically or even legally ask for more information.

TROUBLESHOOTING TOOLS

Let's say you've checked in with yourself and identified an issue. Are you able to self-soothe as your first line of defense? Rituals and routines are the go-to soothers to boost your Emotional Wellness in a time of need. These are self-care tools that you establish ahead of time and that you can put to use quickly when you need 'em to get yourself back in action. Sure, just playing hooky every once in a while and winging a spontaneous night or day off sounds like fun, and it is. But, being too unstructured with your self-care may have been what got you to the point of troubleshooting in the first place.

CREATE YOUR OWN RITUALS

No, I'm not talking about breaking out the candles and crystals here. The kind of rituals I'm talking about creating are unique to *you*. With mindful repetition, they offer comfort and familiarity to even the craziest of days, serving as an antidote to anxiety and stress.

Think of rituals like daily gifts to yourself (and, sure, you can give yourself candles and crystals but only if you want to). You can give yourself anything you want, the possibilities are truly endless: making your bed meticulously, steeping tea after dinner, or going to the infrared sauna every Tuesday. They can be anything that truly, when no one else is watching, tickles your self-care fancy. Here's what some other Super Women turn to:

Laverne Cox, actress and LGBTQ activist, is a fan of somatic therapy (that taps into the "somatic awareness"

I mentioned around intuition). This is a combination of talk therapy and physical movement to help ease stress.

Amy Tan, the author of *The Joy Luck Club*, finds her joy in rock balancing. By which I mean literally balancing rocks on top of each other. She says that while it seems impossible, every rock, no matter how uneven, can balance—you just have to find its balancing point.

Stacey Bendet, Alice + Olivia designer, does an hour of third- or fourth-series ashtanga (read: super advanced) yoga . . . at 4:45 AM.

A ritual also doesn't need to be something you do; it can be something you say. Perhaps you implement a ritual of telling your child one reason you're proud of them over breakfast or your partner three things you love about them before you go to bed. Some couples create more formal weekly check-ins complete with spreadsheets (swoon!) and calendar invites. A consistent ritual that's special to you can give you something to look forward to and count on in any relationship, including the one with yourself, which tends to keep it moving in the right direction.

ROCK A ROUTINE

Just as you'd learn choreography for a dance routine, you need choreography for your life routine as well. Part of setting boundaries for self-care is carving out a space for yourself, and the easiest way to do that is with a morning and evening routine that lets you start and end the day focusing on, well, you. Of course, there's always improvisation in a performance. You could slip, or forget one of your lines, or there could be a glitch with the music. Same with life. But, if you have a foundation to fall back on, you'll be more likely to recover quickly.

Rise and Shine

Your morning routine sets the tone for the rest of your day. I can't emphasize enough how important it is. It's easy to hit the snooze button; you're the boss of your own life, and you're okay with it, right? But you shouldn't be okay with it—because languishing in bed instead of grabbing the day by the balls is hurting your business, whether you work for yourself or someone else.

Tell me if this sounds familiar:

You wake up and check your phone. Check texts. Look at emails. Try to weed through shopping stuff to get to important work stuff but then stop at some of the shopping stuff. Head over to Instagram. Like some posts. See who liked your posts. See what your ex is liking. Look at some news. Go back and refresh Instagram. Maybe look at Facebook. And so on, until you've spent fifteen minutes staring at your phone before even getting out of bed. Or . . . maybe thirty. True? Yeah, been there.

But instead of holding a bright light four inches away from your eyeballs a split second after they open, maybe just . . . don't.

What if your morning looked like this, instead?

You wake up and turn off the alarm on your iPod touch

or, gasp, alarm clock. You stretch. You get up and make some coffee. You sit down with your coffee and maybe write in your gratitude journal, identifying what you're grateful for today and what would make the day awesome. Then you breathe and do a brief meditation exercise, if you're into that sort of thing, or just look outside and observe the world waking up. You shower and do bathroom things. You get dressed. You make breakfast. And then, when you *do* finally open your phone or desktop, you scroll for major headlines, emails, and texts—in that order. You don't open Instagram or its many social media cousins. Like, at all (at least until later in the day).

The first scenario, the one that starts with a screen full of information beaming into my face immediately upon waking up, used to be my exact morning "routine." The second scenario, where I allow my mind and body to wake up and energize first, and I open my phone last, is pretty close to my current routine. The hard and fast parts of my routine now are: 1) waking up with an alarm on something other than a phone, because if it's on my phone, not only will that siren screen be too tempting first thing in the morning, but I'll also play on it at night (and lose track of time searching makeup tutorials), 2) writing in my gratitude journal, to begin the day with intention and on a thankful note, and 3) completing all of the other morning things I need to do for that day *before* I look at my phone.

Until I got the hang of it, I was strict about the exact order my routine followed. And of course I learned to make adjustments, like for when I travel or stay at someone else's home, or if I'm not feeling well. I promise you'll get used to not checking your phone as soon as you wake up. Once I saw how it made me feel, I made a commitment to myself to stick to at least those three things no matter what.

Now, your turn. Outline whatever morning routine you want, just as long as you make it your ritual and stick to it unless there's a really good reason not to. My baseline suggestions are:

- *Use an alarm.* We talked about getting an actual alarm, that's not on your phone, back in Step 7. Now, set it to go off at roughly the same time every day. And even more ideal would be if that time came after seven to eight hours of sleep. You can try a sunrise alarm, which I particularly enjoy because it mimics the effect of the sun rising, increasingly brightening your bedroom until you wake up naturally.

- *Do some sort of gratitude thing.* It can be writing, saying a prayer, and/or some meditative thing, whether it's a formal one or one you come up with yourself. It's easy to create a meditation (see Step 9); I like sitting on the fluffy shag rug in my living room and taking four-second inhales followed by four-second exhales, repeat, for about five minutes, or until I feel awake. Your meditation can be washing your hands, as long as you are only focused on washing your hands. It could be knitting. It's anything that gets you out of your head and away from all the thoughts of things you need to do that day.

- *Forget the phone.* Try not to look at your phone for as long as possible, and when you do, limit your time on it. Better yet, schedule a specific window for it. And yes, I know you're kinda a big deal, but no one

is such a big deal that they can't unplug long enough
to recharge.

Nighty Night

I know, I know, you want to seize the day *and* the night. But the
best way to do so is to seize some time for yourself at either end,
and set the tone for productivity in your waking *and* dream-
ing hours. So, your bedtime routine is just as important as your
morning one.

Here's my former nighttime routine:

It's nine o'clock and I've had a glass or two of wine but
haven't eaten dinner yet, so I order takeout. When it
comes, I mindlessly eat while I'm on the computer "doing
work"—aka online shopping and refreshing Twitter. Then
I agonize over what happened that day, which drives me
to try to smother any shame or guilt I have with almost
a whole pint of ice cream. Then I feel *bad* about eating
basically a whole pint of ice cream, which only happened
because I was mindlessly bobbing around the interwebs
and not even looking at the spoon—and I crawl onto the
couch, scrolling through Instagram, and feel even worse
looking at beautiful, skinny people and their beautiful,
amazing lives. Then I get into my jammies and get under
the covers . . . with my phone, sending emails and doing
a little more online shopping. Just as I'm drifting off, I
remember that I didn't wash off my makeup, so I get up
and go to the bathroom (with my phone) to wash my
face, which wakes me back up, then I get back into bed

(still with my phone). Finally, when I've officially seen the whole internet, I go to sleep, at midnight or maybe later. But just before I do, I set an alarm (on my phone) for as late as I can while still making it humanly possible to arrive on time for my first meeting, plugging in my phone within arm's reach so that I can check it even when I get up to go to the bathroom in the middle of the night.

Did any of that sound familiar?

What if your night looked like this, instead?

You eat dinner around the designated time you established on your schedule back in Step 6. You never eat alone. Now, that doesn't mean you need to hit the town. But it means that you are fully present with your dining companion (even if it's yourself) and eating mindfully instead of shoveling food in your mouth while scrolling through your phone. After dinner, you watch thirty minutes of your favorite show, or take your dog for a walk. Whatever this evening activity is, you choose it with the purpose your time deserves. Then, you take a few minutes to write down your goals for the following day in *The Super Woman Journal*, another journal, or an index card—whatever does it for you—so that you don't have to obsess over them while you're trying to fall asleep. (Plus, setting those intentions ahead of time makes you more likely to follow through the next day.) Next, do whatever little bathroom routine you like. I'm gonna channel Super Woman Rachel Hollis for a moment and say girl, wash your face; it's good for your skin and a nice "signal" to your body and mind of the transition from day to night. Then, after plugging in your phone in another room (I like to leave mine in the kitchen, right next to the coffee-maker), get your booty into bed. Read something sooth-ing, like poetry or an old favorite. It calms you down and makes your eyes tired, as they should be at this time of day. Zzzzzzzzzz.

Everybody talks about how important it is to start the day off right, but setting up a strong nighttime flow is even more important because it closes out your day on a high note *and* sets you up for success the following day. Of course, sometimes you need a night off to put the goal-setting aside, have some fun, or just relax. But that doesn't mean you can't stick to the basic structure of your daily routine (like washing your face when you get home from happy hour and leaving your phone in the other room before you go to bed). After all, a well-deserved night off should be an opportunity to recharge, not an excuse to derail your productivity the following day.

Now, outline your *own* night. Yes, there are a lot of varia-bles—a cranky husband, crying kids, a broken furnace—that can rile you up and keep you from getting to bed. But the more you can stay on track when those things don't happen, the bet-ter you will feel. Remember, a routine means you repeat some-thing. So if your nighttime ritual derails too often (obviously a girl's gotta live sometimes), your morning one will, too—and so will the rest of your day.

Here are some of my best suggestions for making the most of your evening hours:

- *Tidy up.* Take a few minutes to clean up, whether it's your room, your desk, or loading the dishwasher. An organized space gets you in a better headspace to keep your time organized as well.

- *Take a bath.* Dodie Smith, one of my favorite children's book authors (hello, *The Hundred and One Dalmatians!*), once said that "Noble deeds and hot baths are the best cures for depression." I agree. A bath will help sore muscles, clear congestion, and help you detox your body and your mind. Don't have a tub? Fill a large bowl with warm water and a few tablespoons of Epsom salts for a spa-worthy foot soak. Ahh.

- *Go dark.* Research has shown again and again that we sleep best in total darkness, so make sure your bed is facing away from any windows if possible, or look into buying blackout shades. If you are restless, try using a white noise app to relax and block out street sounds. You don't need me to tell you about the many benefits of a good night's sleep. But studies show that routine sleep behaviors, not just the amount of time you sleep (BTW, seven hours and six minutes is the magical number for optimal sleep time), are a huge contributor to Emotional Wellness and your overall health. Lack of sleep is linked to stroke, heart attack, and depression. Super Women deserve to live long lives, so we can all grow up to be the real-life *Golden Girls*. (And, yes, we can all be Blanche.)

According to the Cleveland Clinic, being awake for more than sixteen hours straight decreases your performance as much as if your blood alcohol level were .05 percent (the legal limit is .08 percent). Got that hangover feeling after not sleeping well? Well, it's real. Your body thinks it's drunk!

FYI

A routine is just another kind of ritual that you perform for yourself every day. Like many spiritual rituals honor a higher power, your own rituals are a way to honor yourself and tap into your superpowers. In the same way we talked in the last step about cleaning up your side of the street as you build healthy relationships, it's important to get your house in order with consistent self-care as you build a healthy relationship with *yourself*—before going on to build your empire.

IF A DAY ISN'T ENOUGH

Of course, twenty-four hours or a weekend to yourself is nice, but sometimes it's not enough. Just like a sick day won't actually "cure" your cold, a mental health day might not cure whatever led you to take that day off in the first place. Sometimes, of course, a day or two to take care of yourself and catch your breath is all you need. If it's a temporary fry you are feeling, a mental health day should make you feel 30–50 percent better. If you feel 0 percent better, it may signal that there is something more serious going on, and you need more time to address it.

WHEN A SITUATION BECOMES A CONDITION

My family didn't believe in mental health issues, even though they run in our blood, going back generations. They thought seeing a psychiatrist was weak. I grew up thinking extreme mood disorders and trauma were normal, and treatment was out of the question.

Today, I've broken that cycle. I did it quietly for myself through intense trauma therapy (BTW, "It's a good day for trauma therapy," said no one, ever, but I stuck with it) and now I'm doing it out loud with you. Mental illness is not weakness. When situational depression turns into chronic depression, it's a disorder, not a decision. And, I promise, it's not contagious. While illness is never a choice, your response to it is. Bias is. Stigma is. Kindness is. And I hope *that's* contagious. (For more mental health resources, see the section in the back of the book.)

FYI

As history shows, mental health issues are no barrier to strength and greatness: Martin Luther King Jr. allegedly suffered from chronic depression, as did Winston Churchill and Abraham Lincoln. In fact many artists, executives, and other game-changers have credited a close connection with deep emotions for their resonance with an audience.

Notable people who have come out talking about their mental health struggles include:

- Halle Berry
- Mandy Moore
- Demi Lovato

- Sheryl Crow
- Ellen DeGeneres
- Cara Delevingne
- Catherine Zeta-Jones

"Skills not pills" is a phrase I heard often at the various behavioral classes I've taken. It's a cute saying and also an admirable goal. One of the reasons I wanted to write this book is that the skills for developing and maintaining Emotional Wellness are not taught in school, left off the curriculum in much the same way as personal finance and business basics.

However, there is no shame in the medicine game. In the wise words of Kristen Bell: "You would never deny a diabetic his insulin. Ever. But for some reason, when someone needs a [selective] serotonin [reuptake] inhibitor, they're immediately 'crazy.'" One in nine Americans are on some kind of psychiatric drug, mostly antidepressants. For women in their forties and fifties, that number jumps to one in four. So, whether you're on meds every day long term, just as needed, or for a short period of time, you've got plenty of company. Kristen and I are right here with you.

CONFESSIONS
OF A SUPER WOMAN

The Doctor Is In

I was in my midtwenties when I had my first major episode of situational depression. I'd had similar but less intense episodes throughout my life, times when I couldn't get out of bed for days at a time, or would find myself crying uncontrollably for no apparent reason, or sabotaging close relationships over small, seemingly petty things. But this time, after calling out of work for three consecutive days, I finally realized that maybe I was facing something that was bigger than me.

I've always tried to take medicine only when I really need it. I think this stems from growing up with my doctor father, who literally overmedicated himself to death. So, if I have a headache, I'll drink a ton of water and lie down before popping any pills. Can't sleep? I turn to teas. Scratchy throat? Oil of oregano is my go-to. You get the point. In general, I've always had this idea that I'm tough enough to tough it out. So, as you might imagine, it took a lot to make me consider that I might need psychiatric medication.

I confided in a friend that I thought I needed medication. She gave me the name of "a guy" to see. A psychiatrist.

Getting ready for my first appointment, I was tempted to wear a trench coat and dark sunglasses. I was so embarrassed. I had convinced myself that seeking help was synonymous with being weak. And that if anyone knew I was in over my head and couldn't handle it on my own, I would be exposed for what I felt I was: an imposter.

When the doctor asked me what was going on, I was too much of a mess to put my emotions into words. At the time, I didn't even have the vocabulary to talk about my mental health symptoms. Even if I had, I probably would have been too ashamed to tell him, or to use words like "post-traumatic stress disorder," even though intellectually I knew that treating me was his job, and he had probably seen just about everything in my realm of suffering and beyond.

Instead, I said: "I think I need medicine. Everything hurts."

"What hurts?" the doctor asked in a calm, measured, very shrink-like voice.

"My head; my thoughts, I think. I'm so sad and I can barely get up in the morning and it's really affecting my work. I think I need medication," I repeated, not looking him in the eye. "Can you help me?"

He paused. "I can, but I need a little more background information."

I couldn't give him much; I spent the next hour stuttering through basically the same line over and over again with long awkward pauses: "I think I need medicine. Everything hurts."

When our time was up, I left with two medications: Lexapro and Seroquel—one to address ongoing depression and anxiety and the other for "emergencies." I doubt I used them right, because the side effects were gnarly. Headaches, nausea, sweating through my clothes so that I'd sometimes have to change before going on TV. I was supposed to go back to the psychiatrist for a follow-up appointment. But I never did. Side effects aside, the meds worked. My mood became more stable, and I was able to go back to work, more focused than ever. And then I felt like I knew the magic trick to deal with whatever came my way.

I didn't. The decision to seek medication was the right one. And not seeking therapy to talk through whatever the hell it was that I was medicating in the first place was the wrong one. I quit taking the meds after a few months once I felt better, and I thought I was done with the whole thing.

I wasn't. A year or so later, I had another depressive episode. I was like, "Ugh . . . what's the name of those magic pills again?" I thought I would just have a doctor friend sketchily prescribe them for me, and my mind would clear right up again, like a UTI. Until I could get the prescription, I took my friend's antidepressants (which, knowing now how dangerous that is for your body and mind, is really alarming). I just assumed all were created equal, and they were basically different brand names for the same thing.

They weren't. Rather than stabilizing my mood, my friend's meds just made me more emotional and lethargic. Not all medications are created equal because not all mental health issues are created equal. And what I'd come to learn in the years that followed, after I finally started taking better care of myself, is that not all psychiatrists are created equal, either. It's like finding a personal trainer; you might have to go through a few until you find one who fits your style and needs. This person should be a regular part of your life, not just someone you reach out to when things are going south. Once you've found the right person, finding the right medications usually involves a similar kind of trial and error. Eventually, after finding a psychiatrist I actually trusted, who (bonus!) was also an excellent therapist, I found a combination of medications that worked for me—sans nasty side effects—and a medical professional who monitored me.

At first, almost every time I picked up my meds at the pharmacy, I felt awkward and ashamed. I would take the pills out of their orange prescription bottles and transfer them into a generic Tylenol container, worried that someone would see the label and Google what it was that I was taking.

It wasn't until I started looking at my mental health like I would any other health issue that the shame and barriers that stood in the way of me getting better came down piece by piece. I came to understand that mental illness was not something to be embarrassed about or "tough out." I know now that I really am as tough as it gets—tough enough to ask for help.

A word of caution, however: Antidepressants are not "happy" pills. I should know; I've taken many different ones through the years. But I still didn't fully grasp this for a long time. Antidepressants are like floaties to get you across the pool safely, without drowning. Most antidepressants will help get you from the deep end back to the shallow end, where you can stand up on your own. That shallow end is where everyone starts. Making your way out of the pool altogether to a calm, dry, happy place is up to you.

The way to get out of feeling like you're in a constant state of triage mode is to practice self-care on the regular. There is a reason yoga is called a "practice." You don't just go to one class and become a yogi master. You don't nail a perfect Bird of Paradise bind the first try (trust me, I've tried . . . and met the mat fast). If you want to be great at anything, you can't try it once and then peace out. Similarly, Emotional Wellness isn't something you achieve and then cross off your to-do list. You have to check it (and yourself). Every. Damn. Day.

BOTTOM LINE

Conventional Wisdom: I'm feeling pretty happy, so I'm fine.

Well, mazel tov. But when you're feeling good is the perfect time to ride the momentum and work on yourself *more*, not less. The more Emotional Wellness you put in the bank, the richer in happiness you'll be in the long run.

Conventional Wisdom: Routines are for the military and old people. YOLO!

Wrong-o. Setting, and then sticking to, a regular morning and evening routine is just about as boss a move as they come. After all, our strongest habits start at home. Studies have shown that leaders who practice daily rituals are more productive—and ultimately more successful. Drawing a line around space and time just for you sets the tone for your day in the morning and your dreams at night. Bookend your day with self-care—and look for opportunities to check in with yourself throughout the day—and you'll find success in the waking hours in between.

Conventional Wisdom: The solution to mental illness is mental toughness.

Would you ever tell someone with cancer to just "tough it out" and get on with their lives? No. I'm all about fortifying your Emotional Wellness with tools to keep you on track when times get tough, but some illnesses—whether they are mental or physical—are out of your control. So, before you get out of control, be tough enough to seek the help and resources you need to get well.

Conventional Wisdom: I can't use a sick day if I'm not sick.

Good health is not just physical, it's also mental. And if you are not in tip-top mental shape, you are about as effective as you would be if you had the flu. If you can, take a mental health day when you need it. Better yet, take a week of personal or vacation time. (Here's a sad statistic: Americans leave almost *half* of their paid vacation days on the table each year.) Your brain will benefit from the new perspective, and your colleagues will appreciate not being exposed to any germs or bad vibes. I know I would. It's your time to take, so take it. And set the tone for others around you to do the same.

STEP

12

BE YOUR OWN HERO

Putting (and Keeping) Yourself Together

Becoming a Super Woman doesn't mean you won't have unsuper days, or weeks, or even months. And while it would be awesome if this book had the power to vanquish every battle you are fighting, the truth is there will always be a battle of some sort, and another battle waiting behind it. Being a Super Woman isn't about calling it a victory and hanging up your cape. It's about living with your battle wounds proudly displayed and feeling strong enough to live a full life, even if that means you risk adding more scars. They just show the world that you're stronger than whatever it is that tried to hurt you. My goal is that you become your own hero when you need it, find your own superpowers, and ultimately win your own war.

This isn't some rah-rah Disney movie ending. You aren't "fixed" or "saved" or "better" just because you've made it to the final step in this book. You are the same super you—just more so, because you have improved skills and new tools. My hope now is that you've learned to embrace exactly who you are in all your perfectly imperfect glory, ditching the endless pursuit of perfection in favor of the daily commitment to progress.

Throughout this book we have rethought and reframed . . . everything: from what it means to "have it all," to achieving balance, to managing our time and protecting our energy. In this step, we're going to flip the script one last time and talk about harnessing the power of the crises that will inevitably find us throughout our lives and owning them as part of our story we tell ourselves and the world.

TURN PAIN INTO GAIN

The Chinese word for "crisis" includes the character for "opportunity." You can't choose the crises you face, but you can control what you do with the opportunity to learn from them. Similarly, you can't choose what pains you, but you can choose how to look at and handle that pain.

As the famed poet Rumi says, "The wound is the place where light enters you." We are conditioned to slap a Band-Aid on our wounds. But, instead, what if we exposed them? Aired them out? Like surface wounds, they might just heal faster when they are not all bandaged up and drowning in Neosporin. Wounds are nothing to be embarrassed of or to hide. We all have them. And our wounds are unique to us, therefore they are sacred. The term "sacred wounds" is sometimes used to refer to emotional wounds that you give love and compassion to rather than try to get rid of.

I get it, the idea of trying to make friends with your pain sounds . . . painful. But when you don't listen to pain, it goes deeper, lasts longer, and has the power to take you down. It's only when you acknowledge it that *you* hold the power.

Pain's three greatest powers are:

1. *Catharsis*. There's science that shows us that crying actually does make us feel better. That's because tears contain leucine enkephalin—a natural painkiller.

2. *Contrast*. Nothing lets you feel the highs of joy more fully than experiencing the lows of pain. This is the concept of duality. Yin and yang. Ease and dis-ease. What is joy without pain? No one appreciates spring more than those who have lived through a long, cold winter.

3. *Catalyst*. As terrible as it might feel, pain can be the greatest catalyst for change. You may know, deep down, that you need to make a change—but sometimes it takes pain to kick your ass into actually doing it. And change only happens when the discomfort of the familiar outweighs the fear of the unknown.

When you're hurting, it's tempting to think you can power through the pain instead of addressing it, either by ignoring it or by numbing it away with unhealthy habits. I had always been a big fan of this option, choosing to distract myself with work instead of facing a painful scenario. The more of a mess I was on the inside, the more I worked on making my outside shine. Chasing my next work triumph kept me busy and let me pretend I was in control. But I wasn't.

On my journey to becoming a Super Woman, I had to confront these behaviors and stop avoiding my pain. I started by saying to myself, "No more hiding, distracting, or pretending. Look your pain in the face and ask it what it's trying to tell you."

Well, my pain told me that there are things I can control and things I can't, even when I do all the "right" things. My pain taught me that if I could accept the things I can't control, then I would have more mental, physical, and emotional energy for those that I *can*. Now, I have to continually try to teach myself the "wisdom to know the difference," as the line goes in the "Serenity Prayer." I'm not religious, but you don't have to be for this prayer to resonate with you, too:

> *God grant me serenity*
> *to accept the things I cannot change;*
> *The courage to change the things I can;*
> *And the wisdom to know the difference.*

There is something universal about the prayer's celebration of our own potential and limits. But most people will only be able to recite to that point whether they know it from AA, Al-Anon, other recovery programs, or popular culture (like Kurt Vonnegut's *Slaughterhouse Five* or the movie *Flight*). But take a look at the next three lines:

> *Living one day at a time;*
> *Enjoying one moment at a time;*
> *Accepting hardships as the pathway to peace*

For me, these words are a reminder that pain can lead to peace, in whatever way you define it, be it happiness, fulfillment, or balance. Ignoring your pain might feel blissful in the moment, but embracing it is what will let you transcend it long-term. Knowing your pain and using it to help you heal might be the greatest superpower of them all.

THE POWER OF NEGATIVE THINKING

Yes, of course I know we talked about the power of *positive* thinking in Step 9, but focusing on the positive doesn't work *all* the time. Strategically tapping into your painful thoughts can sometimes work better. Listening to your negative thinking is one of the most powerful ways to turn and stare it down.

During my darkest times, trying to force my attention *away* from my negative thoughts only reminded me that they were there. (Quick: don't think about a polar bear . . . are you thinking of one?!) So, instead, I acknowledged the fears that drove my scary thinking. Fully entertaining my "worst-case scenarios" was the only thing that motivated me to keep them from materializing.

When I hit rock bottom, I felt crippled. The idea of doing anything besides sleeping and moping around was unbearable. As for taking care of myself, I only wanted to entertain quick fixes, like watching a Madea movie or shopping online. So how did I go from Tyler Perry marathons to writing a book about the career benefits of solid Emotional Wellness? Well, for starters, when I found myself at my lowest point, my daily goals were super small. Go outside. Call a friend. Take a shower. Down a shot of apple cider vinegar. That was it.

I'd try to give myself a pep talk every morning: "Lapin, today all you have to do is go on the treadmill for five minutes. That's it. You don't even have to run; you can walk. Just MOVE. That's the one thing you have to do today." Anyone can hop on the treadmill for five minutes, right?! I just had to get up and move. Easy.

And yet . . . I didn't do it.

It's like what happens when you ask someone with all the free time in the world to get something done. It doesn't get done. Without a deadline or any sort of structure, there's no urgency. So, I tweaked my daily pep talk to something with a little less . . . pep, adding a lot more urgency by putting one of my fears front and center.

I started saying stuff like this: "Remember the psych ward, Lapin? How many treadmills were there? Oh, really, none?? Well, get your booty on that treadmill for just five minutes and maybe you won't have to go back there. Ever."

Yep. Scared. Straight. Reminding myself of the worst-case scenario gave myself something to work not just toward, but also against. Instead of assuming I was going to get it done like a rock star, I reminded myself that I was the "Fall Risk" I told you about in Step 1. The more I imagined my world getting rocked again, the harder I worked to stabilize it.

Then, if my goal for the day involved going outside or working out, I would leave my sneakers by the door before I went to bed. Socks and all. If it was about going away somewhere, I would book a flight right away. Once I got some momentum going, I brought in more goals and responded better to the "pep" in my talk. But when the positive was hard to see, the talks I gave myself that were rooted in pain gave me the push I needed to find it again.

Stoicism is an ancient Greek philosophy that teaches self-control over emotions (it's from this philosophy that we get the English word "stoic"). Many of its teachings focus on "pre-meditation of evils," or purposely focusing on the worst-case scenario. By visualizing that, you tend to a) conclude that you can cope even if it *does* actually happen, and b) motivate yourself to appreciate what you have, whether it's your freedom or your loved ones, as you recognize that they are ephemeral.

FYI

Use negative self-talk judiciously—and remember, there's a difference between self-motivation and self-hate. It isn't intended to freak you out, put you down, or give you anxiety. It's meant to make you realize how good you already have it, how strong you already are. For me, focusing on the dark for a period of time made me want to live in the light even more.

If your negative thinking does start to make you feel more afraid than motivated, list out those fears. Is your "worst-case scenario" that you get fired? Write out what you would do if that happens. Would you live off savings? Move in with a friend? Whatever you would do, the point is, *you would be okay*. Maybe not great, or even good, but still alive, right? If I actually *do* have another breakdown (which I'm not planning on doing, but you never know), I will be okay, too.

We are only born with two innate fears: a fear of loud noises and a fear of falling down. All other fears are learned through the shit we go through, aka our pain. I think of my fear(s) as an acronym: False Evidence Appearing Real. Or, more eloquently put by the famous Stoic philosopher Seneca: "we suffer more in imagination than reality." Fear happens. Use it to become fearless.

PLANT FLOWERS, PULL WEEDS

There's no sense in waiting until you are on the other side of pain to start cultivating joy. Relishing in and savoring joyful moments will help counteract and balance those of suffering. As my super wise gardener says, "You can plant flowers *and* pull weeds." It's not one or the other. You must still live your life while you heal.

While pulling weeds, or breaking unhealthy habits, is no fun, planting flowers, or creating healthy habits, can be even harder. According to a groundbreaking study from University College London, it can take an average of sixty-six days to create a solid habit. One of the most successful ways to do that is to break the habit down into three stages: 1) the cue that reminds you to do the action, 2) the action itself, and 3) the reward for doing the action.

We often forget about the reward part, which is a mistake. After all, what would you willingly do over and over again without ever getting anything back? Nada. So, let's say you want to establish the healthy habit of working out every morning. The *cue* would be setting the coffeemaker timer to go off first thing, so that you smell that aroma at the time you plan to go. The *action* is going to the gym. And the *reward* would be getting a yummy almond butter smoothie afterward.

This process rewires your brain to *want* to keep sticking to the new habit. When we consciously create a new habit, we are harnessing the power of our unconscious mind to create new neural pathways to make it stick. (BTW, 95 percent of what we do is done by our subconscious, which is why we don't think about brushing our teeth or driving a car.) And when that new habit finally sticks, it becomes permanent. "Neurons that fire together, wire together" is just neurologist-speak for the simple truth that what sticks keeps sticking.

You can break an unhealthy habit using the same formula, keeping the same cue, but changing the reward. So let's say you want to stop diving into work (habit) to numb your pain of losing a loved one (reward) that gets triggered every time you hear a particular song (cue). Then the next time you hear that song (cue), try to do something else, like call a friend or take a walk to reflect (habit) and assuage the pain (reward).

Of course, deep-rooted habits come with multiple cues and rewards every day. Finding all of them isn't easy. But your new landscape is worth the work.

FYI

Ayurveda is one of the world's first medical systems and healing methods, originating in India more than three thousand years ago. It rests on the belief that the mind affects what happens in your body more than anything else. Ayurvedic wisdom tells you to think of yourself as a tree—if the tree is wilting, where do you put the fertilizer? Not on the leaves, but on the roots.

Obviously I want a beautiful garden as much as you do. And as much as I want mine to flourish all year round, I only set myself up for more pain if I expect it to. A lot of pain stems from setting unrealistic expectations and then falling short. Growth comes from keeping expectations grounded and looking at any extra bloom as a bonus.

YOU ARE THERE

I used to say "when I get there . . ." I'll be balanced. "When I get there . . ." I'll be happy. My brain never let me get to the other side of balance or happiness because there was always another "there" there.

I got all the things I thought I wanted. My dream job was to be an anchor on CNN. Check. Then my dream job was to have my own network business show. Check. Then it was to have a bestselling book. Check. And then it was another. Check. The more I checked off, the less balanced or happy I was. I never got *there*.

I don't usually look to Jim Carrey for inspirational quotes, but he said something that drives this point home: "I think everybody should get rich and famous and do everything they ever dreamed of so they can see that it's not the answer." It's true. I started this book by telling you *there is no external solution for an internal problem*. By now I hope you know that.

None of the accomplishments I achieved, or the money I earned, made me feel like I was ever "there." It was only once I decided I *was* there that I could be balanced and be happy. And you are right *there* with me.

CLAIM YOUR BAGGAGE

It has been said that if you get a group of people to put all of their problems in the middle of the room, once they see what others have, they will almost always grab their own back. We all have baggage. Some of yours might be heavy, but don't forget that somewhere out there in the baggage claim of life, someone else's is even heavier. Remembering that often gives me the strength to carry my own baggage when it feels too heavy to shoulder. It also reminds me of the support we give to ourselves and others when we put our baggage out there.

In order to leave the hospital on my own, I had to sign up for a "dialectical behavioral therapy," or "DBT," intensive course. It was a four-hour class, three days per week at an outpatient psychiatric program two hours away. But I would have traveled much farther for the emotional mileage I got out of it.

The concept of "dialectics" (the "D" in "DBT") is the idea that opposing thoughts can exist side by side, and that even if two things are in opposition, they can be true at the same time. It teaches you to visualize your life like having a picnic on the grass. The dirt. The bugs. The sun. The leaves. You can't only accept the sun. You can't only accept the bugs, either. You accept the whole scene, complete with its awesome and not awesome parts.

Similarly, you can say "I'm angry about my job" *and* also "I love the work I do." You can "be happy" and also "have a shitty day." These statements seem to be in opposition, but both are true and both exist. One is not "more true" or "less true."

The truth is, you can be a paradox. You don't have to sugarcoat or oversimplify what you feel or who you are. I don't.

I am both strong and sensitive. Ambitious and relaxed. Social and a loner. Or, as Alanis Morissette would say, "I'm free but I'm focused; I'm green but I'm wise; I'm hard but I'm friendly, baby."

And now that we are friends, I hope that, because I have

opened up in this book, you feel ready to be more open, too. To have success in any industry, you have to inspire trust and form connections with others—and it's hard to form a genuine connection when you aren't being honest about who you are. The more you accept that being many seemingly contradictory things at once doesn't make you an imposter, the more real connections you will make with other Super Women who are also both masterpieces and works in progress at the same time.

It's impossible to reach your full potential without honoring your full self and your entire story. You might say, "Yeah, but am I comfortable enough in my own skin to share it?" or "Am I confident enough to own it?" All of that is shame talking. The difference between guilt and shame is that the former asserts "I made a mistake," while the latter asserts "I am a mistake." We all make mistakes, but there is no way, no how, you are anywhere near being one yourself. As Super Woman Brené Brown so eloquently and hilariously says in her mega-popular TED Talk, the cure for shame is vulnerability. You might worry that if you're vulnerable, people will take advantage of you. That's possible. But, if you're not vulnerable, the shame will take advantage of you. That's guaranteed.

Superheroes like Superwoman may assume their identities only in a time of crisis, running off to change in a phone booth, but Super Women wear their capes every day, out in the open. Sometimes we spill coffee on our capes. Sometimes we feel like we can barely get out of bed, much less leap tall buildings in a single bound. But we have the strength to keep moving forward—pursuing progress, not perfection.

When you look at the sum of all your decisions, indecisions, strengths, and areas for growth, what do you get? You get your story as it is told right now. I know you might want to rip out some less-flattering or particularly painful chapters, but don't. Instead, look at them dialectically: with *both* compassion and a desire for change. Forgiveness and tough love. Honoring the old book while writing a new one.

You know I love me a good saying, and I've quoted a lot of them in these last, well, couple hundred pages. But this one is my ultimate favorite, and I have it hanging on my wall right by my bed so that it's the first thing I see when I wake up and the last thing I see before I go to bed: "Everything will be okay in the end. If it's not okay, then it's not the end."

This is the end of my story for now, but it's also just the beginning . . . so, what's your story, Super Woman?

BOTTOM LINE

Conventional Wisdom: Superwoman > Super Woman

Super Woman > Superwoman

EPILOGUE

This book was supposed to come out six months earlier than it actually did. I pushed the date of publication back because I was near relapsing. Yes, here I was, writing a book on balance, and I felt totally imbalanced and near burnout . . . again.

So, I stopped writing and took some time to actually *read* the advice and complete the exercises in the book for myself—all twelve steps. And guess what? After I finished the book, and recommitted to doing the work, I started to feel like myself again. My happiest, most productive and balanced self.

That's how I know it works.

At first, I was embarrassed to be writing a book on balance while feeling like my own life was hanging in it. I felt like a fraud. Everyone I spoke with about the book asked me what my secret was to staying balanced—and I didn't have one.

I had to remember that there is no secret. Balance is a skill. And I have become skilled, not in remaining balanced at all times but in being able to regain my balance when I need to. And as with any skill, even the masters must practice it over and over again to become and stay proficient.

The word "balance" can be both a noun and a verb, a thing and an action, but achieving true Super Woman balance means using it as a verb. It's not something you find once and then stop looking for. It's not a thing that's hiding somewhere. Balance is constantly in motion. It's active—and something in which you must be an active participant. It's something you *do*. All. The. Time.

After getting to the other side of my breakdown, I got cocky and stopped practicing balance as much as I should have. I was feeling good, and forgot I was a "Fall Risk." I quickly slipped back into my old habits—ones that numbed the imbalance but didn't solve it. I went back to thinking that there were external solutions to my internal problems. And, of course, there never are. So I fell.

As much as I shamed myself for slipping, I can't actually blame myself. Like most people, I have a lifetime of unhealthy habits deeply ingrained in my brain. There's even a fancy word for it: "neuroplasticity," which describes the phenomenon that occurs when the things you do over and over again stick and become habits. To ingrain healthy habits instead, I needed to practice *those* for longer than the unhealthy ones, so that they were the stronger pathways in my brain. Sure, I worked on my Emotional Wellness, but not for long enough. It didn't become a habit because I didn't cultivate it continuously; and nothing less than a lifetime is long enough for that. Just as we wouldn't expect to take a break from physical fitness and return to the gym as strong as before, we can't expect to take a hiatus from mental fitness and remain in balance.

It's tempting to stop working on Emotional Wellness, especially during crazy-busy times or when everything seems to be going fine. But here's the thing: Life *constantly* tests us with chaos and change. Just when we think we have it figured out, *bam!* Something unexpected—tragedy, joy, loss, gain—happens. The only thing we can be certain of is uncertainty. And the only thing we can control is how we respond to that uncertainty, which means developing the tools and skills required to regain our balance when we slip.

While writing this book, old demons gave me a test that I didn't pass. But I learned something I'll be able to use for the next test: Between every chaotic event in our lives and our response to it is a space, a gap, where the growth for which we've worked so hard can happen—but only if we let it. That gap allows us to pause and choose whether to keep stepping out of our comfort zone and growing or to go back to our past, familiar ways as soon as things become uncomfortable.

I got stuck in that gap, thinking, *I'll get back to the balance stuff when . . .* , or *I'd be balanced if only . . .* , just to realize all over again that there will always be another "when" and "if only." Balance and chaos happen together. They must, because without each other, they cannot exist.

It is easy to think *I'll be balanced **or** in chaos*. But the harder truth is to know that *I'll be balanced **and also** in chaos*. Accepting and living by that makes you less of a "Fall Risk."

Embrace the power of the paradox. Be proud of how you bridge the gap when tested. It's what separates the women from the Super Women.

RESOURCES

*If you are feeling unsafe or like you might hurt yourself, call the **National Suicide Prevention Lifeline** at **1-800-273-8255**. It is totally confidential, and staffed 24/7 by people who care. Please reach out. The world needs your super self.*

Mental Health Apps

- **Talkspace.** Based on a free consultation, you are matched up with a licensed therapist for remote sessions. There are all kinds of options in terms of the level of service you want to pay for, but the therapy is about *80%* cheaper than it would be IRL. It is also a great choice if you don't quite feel ready for in-person therapy.
- **Happify.** Using techniques from mindfulness and positive psychology, this app helps you fight negative thinking and build happiness and resilience, giving you a happiness "score" you can work to improve over time with games and activities. (86% of users report feeling better after two months!)
- **Headspace** and **Calm** are the go-to apps for

meditation, offering hundreds of meditation and mindfulness sessions as well as relaxation and breathing exercises, and soothing sounds like rain and whatnot.

- **Daily DBT Diary** and **Mindfulness Daily** are great staples for daily journaling, gratitude, and mindfulness practices.

- **Anxiety and Depression Association of America App List.** New mental health apps are coming out all the time—there will probably be a dozen more by the time this book is printed. A good resource is the app directory maintained by the Anxiety and Depression Association of America (https://adaa. org/resources-professionals/mobile-apps-review).

Online Forums and Resources

- **National Alliance on Mental Illness.** A national mental illness advocacy organization, NAMI offers education, support, and even has their own crisis app. Their site has articles, advice, support resources, and personal accounts from people sharing their own stories of battling mental illness, as well as online discussion boards.

- **National Institute of Mental Health.** In depth information on mental health topics, including all the latest news and research (you know how I love me a good study), updates on insurance coverage, and resources.

- Sometimes it's easier to open up to people you can't see, and there are support groups and forums online for just about everything, from panic disorder to trichotillomania (obsessive hair pulling) to infertility. The forums at **PsychCentral** (psychcentralforums. com) are a great place to start, with boards for any issue you can think of, as well as for specific discussion about meds, therapies, and so on. And Google is your friend—do a search for "forum" or "support" and whatever you're struggling with, and I guarantee you'll find a group of other people in the same spot.

Finding a Therapist

- **GoodTherapy.org** and **PsychologyToday.com** have comprehensive directories of mental health professionals in your area, wherever you are. The directories can be filtered and sorted in a dozen ways, and include therapist bios, the type of treatment they provide, the issues they specialize in, as well as information about the kinds of insurance accepted, credentials, and fees.

- **Employee Assistance Programs.** If you work for a big company—or even a small one—chances are you can get free help through your employer. Employee assistance programs (EAPs) usually offer a number you can call to get help with anything from mental health issues to financial or legal problems, and they can often connect you to other resources, like in-person counselors. Check with your HR department if you have one or look at your benefits info. The best part? EAPs are usually administered by a third party and are always completely confidential—your boss won't know anything about it unless you tell her yourself.

- Only psychiatrists or certain nurse practitioners can prescribe medication, but if you're looking for therapy, you have lots of options, from psychologists to family therapists to licensed clinical social workers (LICSWs). You may not think of social workers when you think of therapists, but LICSWs are highly trained and their national average rate is $136 an hour, whereas a psychologist's is $163.

- Just as I advocate negotiating your salary and bills, you can and should negotiate your mental health care. Many providers offer sliding scales based on your income. So, let's say it's $100/session, and you earn $50,000 or less; you may be eligible for a 25% discount (or more). Some insurance companies also allow you to pay your appointment co-pays with the pre-tax income from a Flexible Spending Account (FSA). Ask upfront—and just because there isn't a discount system in place yet doesn't mean there can't be.

IRL Communities

- As with online support forums, in person support groups are out there in droves, for everything from loss to addiction to stress management. Check out the bulletin boards at your gym, library, church, or community center, or look online at your local neighborhood site (like Nextdoor) or in your neighborhood newspaper.

- If you are dealing with addiction or the effects of a loved one who has struggled with addiction, there are Alcoholics Anonymous, Al-Anon, and Adult Children of Alcoholics groups everywhere. (Adult Children of Alcoholics groups often teach DBT-related strategies and are useful for those with trauma—ask me how I know.)
- Hospitals and clinics often offer situation-specific groups for those dealing with certain kinds of losses, for new moms, and so on, but most also have more general offerings as well. If you already see a therapist, their practice may have group therapy sessions covering specific issues or strategies.
- NAMI, mentioned earlier, offers in-person support groups and classes that you can find via their website, and many of the others online resources listed also have sections pointing you in the direction of local groups.

DIY and Destination Retreats and Classes

- When it comes to relieving stress, a yoga class is always an easy choice, but you might also consider looking for a local meditation center. Another great option is a class on "Mindfulness Based Stress Reduction," a course that has a ton of research backing it up and is often found at local wellness centers.
- Try Coursehorse.com to find local classes that let you be meditative without meditating or just spent some quality time with yourself doing something

new—they have everything, from pottery to comedy workshops.

- Whether you're looking to get away or stay in town, Airbnb Experiences is a great resource for all kinds of, well, experiences, from classes to retreats to tours. Whether you want to learn to surf, see a new place through the eyes of a local, or cuddle a bunch of kittens (seriously) there is something for everyone.

- And of course, if you're looking for an experience or community away from home, be sure to download *The Super Woman Guide to Trips, Treatments, and Therapies for Balance on a Budget*, available now at TheSuperWomanGuide.com. It brings together all of the exclusive knowledge and tricks that I learned from classes, experts, and healers all over the world—no wallet or passport required.

CAN'T STOP, WON'T STOP

I f you're looking for *more* ways to become a Super Woman, a) you're my kind of woman, and b) head over to www.becomingsuperwomanbook.com where I've got you covered with plenty of URL support for your IRL journey.

There you'll find links to the following tools:

- **The Balance School**, a video masterclass on banishing burnout, staving off breakdowns and achieving lasting balance taught by yours truly. It includes interviews with some of the badass Super Women who have endorsed the book, interactive worksheets and quizzes. It also has a community forum where you can chat with other Super Women just like you.
- **The Super Woman Quiz,** an assessment of your own individual superpowers with customized advice and personalized recommendations for staying balanced on your way to becoming a Super Woman.
- *The Super Woman Guide to Trips, Treatments, and Therapies for Balance on a Budget,* a free e-book

that chronicles some of my adventures on my quest for the answers to the questions that prompted me to write this book. It also tells you how much everything I did cost and the gist of what I learned so you don't have to pay the same amount to get the benefit! You're. Welcome.

- *The Super Woman Journal,* my solution to staying balanced every day. It has daily prompts to help you assess what needs to be done and prioritized based on your goals along with exercises to help you feel inspired (and sane) each morning and night. If you're ready to stop measuring your success using someone else's ruler, but don't know how . . . *this* is how.
- **The Super Woman Squad**, our ambassador program. The women who are part of it enjoy early access to my launches, exclusive webinars, free shiz and a solid network of like-minded Super Women from around the world. Apply to join today.

And, if you want to track my adventures and misadventures real-time or join me at one of my next events, follow @nicolelapin on all the social media platforms you can think of.

INDEX

ACKNOWLEDGMENTS

There is a scene at the end of the movie *Tombstone* where Wyatt Earp's character says all he ever wanted was "just to live a normal life." And Val Kilmer's character Doc replies, "There is no normal life . . . It's just life. Get on with it."

My life has not been "normal." No one's is. But I wouldn't have been able to "get on with it" without the following people:

Steve Troha, my fearless book agent, for being wind beneath this Super Woman's cape. You have been my champion when others haven't. I thought we were going to stop at one book baby, but look at the family we have created together. I couldn't have birthed the one book—let alone three—without you as a partner.

Glenn Yeffeth, the visionary of BenBella, for making me a partnership offer I couldn't refuse. You are the CEO every company should have: patient, tough, and fair at the right times. You have innovated in an industry that doesn't see a lot of it. I am glad I was smart enough to say "yes" to working with you and lucky to be part of your vision.

The entire (all female!) BenBella team—including Alexa, Leah, Adrienne, Sarah, Jennifer, Monica, and Alicia—for being rockstars in your respective areas. You listened to every one of my crazy ideas, and you believed in me and them more than they merited at times. You took risks that many wouldn't and chances that most couldn't, always leading with passion over fear. I am so proud to be part of a team of such Super Women.

Jared Greenwald, my super agent, for hustling like no other. You are fierce and fiercely loyal. You are "fully transparent" about everything including your love for that phrase and me. And to be fully transparent back: the feeling is mutual. I wouldn't want anyone else by my side, as my protector and friend, for the adventures (and misadventures) we've gotten into.

Megan Nelson, my marketing queen, for reading my mind and translating it for the world better than I ever can. You are multi-talented in ways that make my head hurt to think about. I can't wait for us to continue to disrupt this industry one GIF at a time—and have a crazy amount of fun doing it.

Sabrina Andersen, my web wizardress, for putting up with me for more than a decade. Your creativity and work ethic are ridiculously strong but nothing compared to the strength in your conviction to always have my back. I trust you with my life (and my passwords, which is basically the same thing).

Elizabeth, Caroline and Tim Stephen, my found family, for treating me as if I were your own. There's no tribe I would rather be part of and no other Thanksgiving table I would rather sit at. Your genuine warmth, support and dependability continue to amaze me. We might not have the same blood, but we are made up of the same moral DNA and that bond is stronger.

Deanna Siller, for always being ready, bag packed, for an adventure. If "woman's woman" were in the dictionary, your picture would be next to it. You are my unbiological sister. I'm not sure which one of us is "dis girl" or "dat girl" but I'll always be whatever girl you need me to be.

Kristy Reed, for listening to me talk in circles about the same thing for hours or days or years and responding with the same sincere Southern sweetness as if it was the first time you were hearing it. You are the only woman I've ever picked up at a bar. Since then, I've loved dancing on them and raising them together.

Sarah Zurell, for always having the right song to play, meme to send, activity to do or comfort food to eat to remind me that "it's gonna be okay." Well, babe, it's gonna be okay. And if it's not okay, I'll ride with you until it is.

Leanne Mai-ly Hilgart, for always having the right nugget of wisdom for every occasion. I'll never know how or why you always answer my call no matter what you have going on to listen to my ramblings and care about my issues as if they were your own. But I'll stop wondering and just keep answering any time you need the same.

Stephanie Abrams, for your compassion, advice and super-long, spot-on motivational texts when I need them most. You have covered countless storms but still have the bandwidth to be shelter in mine and for that I could not be more thankful.

Ellen London, for being the "vegan mac and cheese in my fridge" that I didn't know I needed after that shitty hospital food. You have always been my hero when I couldn't be my own. You have picked me up more than I deserve, been there for me when no one else has and loved me even when I was convinced that I was unlovable. Thank you for being my rock at rock bottom.

A special shout-out to the other Super Women who have helped my cape fly high: Meghan Asha, Rhona Banaquid, Dominique Broadway, Chloe Coscarelli, Liz Dee, Tracy DiNunzio,

Lavinia Errico, Caitlin Fitzpatrick, Kate Garrison, Michelle Gielan, Jessica Gordon, Jennifer Grey, Lena Hall, Hilary Hanson, Jami Kandel, Alex Kopp, Aliza Licht, Tatiana Logan, Christie Marchese, Johnanna Murphy, Lauren Nowell, Daphne Oz, Lisa Oz, Meredith Rollins, Lindsay Samakow, Shachar Scott, Taryn Southern, Paula Sutter, Jaclyn Trop, Baya Voce, Rachel Winnikates, Jessica Yankelunas, Randi Zuckerberg.

To anyone who has ever hurt me—exes, family, former friends—I forgive you and I honor you for making me the person I am today.

And, finally, to *myself*, whom I wouldn't even have thought to acknowledge before writing this book. I'm proud of you for not just making it through hell but for walking out of the flames carrying buckets of water for those still consumed by the fire. You are stronger than you think and braver than you know. Thank you for trying, for failing, and for always sticking with your lifelong pursuit of happiness. Thank you for being my hero when I needed you most.

ABOUT THE AUTHOR

NICOLE LAPIN is the New York Times bestselling author of *Rich Bitch: A Simple 12-Step Plan for Getting Your Financial Life Together . . .Finally* and *Boss Bitch: A Simple 12-Step Plan to Take Charge of Your Career.* Nicole is no stranger to breaking down complex business principles for all to understand, utilizing her signature sassy style. From anchoring business shows on network television, including on CNBC, Bloomberg and CNN, to contributing money reports to TODAY and MSNBC, Nicole has a long history with speaking the language of money fluently, and using that language to empower an entire generation of women to take control of their lives and their finances. Star of the CW's business competition reality show *Hatched*, Nicole helps a fresh wave of entrepreneurs to get their businesses off the ground with smart advice and actionable feedback on their products. She was the first woman to be voted "Money Expert of the Year" and *Redbook* magazine's first-ever monthly money columnist. Nicole graduated as valedictorian from Northwestern University.

"The role of women in the workforce is changing and today women are disrupting the workplace— for the better. Ladies, it's time to disrupt your own industry. **BOSS** BITCH will show you how."

—Sara Blakely, Founder of Spanx

A Sassy and Actionable Guide to Empowering Women to Be the Boss of Their Lives and Their Careers

ALSO BY NICOLE LAPIN

RICH BITCH
A Simple 12-Step Plan for Getting
Your Financial Life Together...Finally

Available in Paperback and E-book

"Let Nicole be the doctor for your financial health and
you will feel better in more ways than you'd think."

—Dr. Oz, host of *The Dr. Oz Show*

Rich Bitch rehabs whatever bad money habits you might have and
provides a plan you can not only sustain, but also thrive on. You won't
feel deprived but rather inspired to go after the rich life you deserve,
and confident enough to call yourself a Rich Bitch.

Available Wherever Books Are Sold